The
Community College
Solution

THOMAS J. SNYDER
President, Ivy Tech

The Nation's Largest Singly Accredited Statewide
Community College System

ACKNOWLEDGMENTS

Special thanks to my wife, my children and my grandchildren, and to my many friends and former colleagues from my days at General Motors and as CEO of Delco Remy, for their never-ending help and support.

DEDICATION

To the 100,214 students who completed their
degrees and certificate programs during my years at
Ivy Tech. Your success means everything to me..

CONTENTS

FOREWORD   i

PREFACE   iii

THE COMMUNITY COLLEGE AT ITS CORE   1

1   Community College Success Stories   2

2   Questions for the College of Your Choice   5

3   Employers Should Value the Two-Year Degree   8

4   Supporting Community College Students   11

5   The Case for Career and Technical Education   15

6   The Benefits of Online Learning   19

COMMUNITY COLLEGES HELP PEOPLE SUCCEED   23

7   A Better Way to Help Low-Income College Students   24

8   Colleges and Returning Vets   28

9   Back to College at 50   31

10   Community Colleges Welcome Career Changers   34

11   Professional Certification from a Community College: 37
A Solution for the Unemployed

12   Mentoring Cultivates College Success   40

13   A Blueprint for Free Community College   43

14   Retirees Return to Community College   48

HELPING AMERICA'S EMPLOYERS   51

15   The Booming Field of Aviation Technology   52

16   Criminal Justice and Community College   55

17   The Hospitality Industry and Community College   58

18   Community Colleges and the Manufacturing Sector   61

19   A Threat to the Backbone of Our Healthcare System: 65
Restricting Access to Nursing

20   Community Colleges and Tech Support   69

21   Community Colleges and Healthcare   73

22   Apprenticeship Programs: An Age-Old Solution to a   77
Contemporary Problem

A FOUNDATION FOR HIGHER EDUCATION   83

23   Community Colleges and College Attainment   84

24   Research Supports Work of Community Colleges   88

25   High School Students Should Earn Credits at   92
Community Colleges

26   Free Community College is a Game Changer   95

27   Community Colleges' Mission to Transfer Students to   98
Four-Year Institutions

28   Remedial Education at Community Colleges   101

COMMUNITY COLLEGES AND THE ECONOMY   105

29   Community College Supports Entrepreneurs   106

30 Community Colleges and the Skills Gap   110

31 Community Colleges and China   114

32 The Contributions of Community Colleges to   117
   Cities and Towns

33 Investing in the American Workforce   120

                         AFTERWORD   123

            FREQUENTLY ASKED QUESTIONS   126

FOREWORD

More than 12 million people attend America's community colleges each year. Thirty-six percent of them are the first generation of their families to attend college; 17 percent are single parents; 12 percent have disabilities.

They enroll for many different reasons. Some – about 41 percent – are first-time freshman starting their college careers; some are high school students seeking advance college credits; others are people well along in their careers acquiring new skills, while still others take programs leading to non-degree certificates in fields such as information technology and emergency medicine.

The "community" in community college is as broadly defined as our nation. Sixty-one percent of Native American undergraduates attend community college, and in fact there are 35 tribal community colleges in the U.S. African Americans are also strongly represented, with 52 percent of black undergraduates studying at a community college, and 57 percent of Hispanics.

America's 1,123 community colleges are financially accessible for virtually everyone – and as you'll see in the following pages, progress is being made in the movement to make tuition free for most students. The average annual tuition and fees at community colleges totaled $3,347 for the 2014-2015 school year, while four-year state colleges charged $9,139.

Community colleges in 2013 awarded 750,399 Associate degrees, and 459,073 certificates for technical and professional programs.

Getting their start in 1901 with the founding of Joliet Junior College in Illinois, in the early 21st century community colleges are essential to America and our economy. On the following pages I lay out why that is so, detail the contributions of community colleges and how they help students and employers, and try to look a bit into the future of this great civic resource.

My hope is to bring community colleges into focus for America, and help the public see the great value of our investment in this vital form of education.

Tom Snyder
President,
Ivy Tech, Indiana

PREFACE

The average U.S. college student now emerges with more than $35,000 in debt after attending a four-year public institution. Overall student debt now exceeds $1.2 trillion, more than the entire country's credit card debt, according to Debt.org.

This crushing obligation often means that graduates have to delay getting married, buying a home or even furthering their education. In addition, students with crushing debt gravitate away from professions like social work and healthcare and focus instead on jobs in technology and the financial services industry.

Financially, our country's education system is in crisis. Soon, only the very wealthy will be able to send their children to a four-year school, and the divide between the middle class and the affluent will become more pronounced. The average college graduate makes 60 percent more in his or her lifetime than a high school graduate. So, higher education is vitally important.

I maintain that community colleges can turn the tide and enable all students, regardless of their socio-economic background, to receive a sound education and get a job with good middle-class wages without going into debt.

We need to change the thinking of parents and guidance counselors that bright students should not enroll at a community college. All students, who want to pursue a four-year degree should consider taking their first two years of coursework at their local community college. They'll get a great education, transferable credits, and it will save them an average of $4,000. Many community college systems, such as Florida's, guarantee a place in one of the state's excellent four-year institutions upon completion of a two-year degree.

We have to re-examine our belief, too, that all students should get a four-year degree. There are many jobs such as a web developer, lab technician, paralegal, occupational therapist and air traffic controller that only require an associate degree with an average starting salary of more than $50,000 per year.

In addition, only a certificate is required to become a welder, EMS personnel, medical billing professional, solar instillation technician, insurance representative, mortgage broker or court reporter. Certificate programs often require passing a national exam, which means that one can be a court reporter or a wind turbine repairperson in any state.

Community colleges have also embraced the apprenticeship model created in Germany, where students are hired by a local business and work while taking classes paid for by their employer at a community college. There are hundreds of these programs in the U.S. with companies such as Siemens, Cummins and Chrysler, among others. And many companies hire their apprentices after they have completed their courses. Community colleges should be part of any city's plan to attract new industry by offering to train workers.

Higher education should be a prudent investment that guarantees a high return. Community colleges are the affordable, practical and proven solution to solving the student debt problem and training our country's future work force. This is the era of the community college – a resource for America that will provide both affordability and excellence for generations to come.

THOMAS J. SNYDER

THE COMMUNITY COLLEGE AT ITS CORE

Community college prepares students to learn, live and work in a diverse and globally competitive environment by delivering professional, technical, transfer and lifelong education. Through affordable, open-access education and training programs, community college enhances the development of America's people and communities and strengthens its economy.

There is no need to graduate with a mountain of debt and no prospect of a job. Community colleges are now the middle class's last hope for a higher education degree.

1 – COMMUNITY COLLEGE SUCCESS STORIES

November 17, 2012

C ollege graduation ceremonies were once a time for celebration. Today, many students receive their four-year degree with more than $80,000 in debt and no prospects of a good job, For the first time, the middle class in this country is faced with the reality that a college education may no longer be an viable financial option.

One group of students who are graduating debt free and finding well-paying jobs are those who attend community colleges. I spoke to dozens of these students as part of research for my book *The Community College Careers Track: How to Achieve the American Dream Without a Mountain of Debt*, which was published in September by Wiley.

What I learned is that whether it is a traditional student or a displaced worker, community colleges offer an opportunity to pursue a higher education degree or a certification program that leads directly to employment. Community colleges work directly with local businesses. They find out what training an employee should have and create a curriculum that meets that demand. Many of the professors actually work in these industries and bring a wealth of knowledge that they pass on to their students.

Many graduates of four-year institution would envy Tricia Jenkins, who graduated from Alvin Community College in Alvin, Texas, with a certificate in court reporting and now earns $78,000 a year working for a legal firm in Houston. The 23-year-old received guidance from her professors, not only with her coursework, but also in preparing for the state professional exam. She paid back her student loan after three months on the job.

Increasingly, businesses are recognizing how valuable their employees are and sending them to a community college for additional training. That was the case for Heather Nauglar of Davison, Michigan, whose employer sent her to Mott Community College in Flint to study electronics. Upon completion of her degree, she will earn upwards of $50,000 as an Electronics Technician.

Pat Cumber, a machinist, was laid off from her job at Mercury Marine in Fond Du Lac, Wisconsin., and decided to pursue her real love – food. The married mother of five enrolled at Fox Valley Tech in Appleton, Wisconsin and earned an Associate degree in Marketing and a certificate in Entrepreneurship. This helped her launch her business Food Tailor, a food truck that serves international cuisine with a home-style flair. Today, while working 30 to 40 hours a week on her food truck, she is pursuing an Associate degree in culinary arts so that she can expand her menu. Her husband works with her and they earn enough to support their family.

What all these community college students have in common is that their educations cost less than $10,000 and lead to well paying jobs that offer an opportunity for advancement. And they were able to pay off their loans. Nursing, culinary arts, technology, law enforcement, and graphic design are all areas of study offered by community colleges, and these industries, among others, are projected to grow substantially in the next decade according to the U.S. Department of Labor.

There is no need to graduate with a mountain of debt and no prospect of a job. Community colleges are now the middle class's last hope for a higher education degree. Federal, state and local governments should support them and businesses need to work with them more closely in the years ahead.

It is time to face the fact that a four-year liberal arts degree may now be a luxury. Community colleges offer their students a more attractive ROI.

Parents and students will find that their local community college often offers a better ROI than four-year colleges.

2 – QUESTIONS FOR THE COLLEGE OF YOUR CHOICE
April 24, 2013

Millions of high school students have now received college acceptance letters. Many middle class Americans will also learn how much financial aid they will receive from these institutions and what they will need to borrow to make up the difference.

As president of Ivy Tech in Indiana, the nation's largest singly-accredited community college system, I recognize that we are in the midst of a college affordability crisis. Students are now graduating with at least $25,000 in debt, loans they can't pay back because they can't get a job. The Consumer Protection Agency estimates that student loan debt exceeds the $1 trillion mark.

Before taking out a student loan, one that it may be impossible to pay back after graduation, I propose that parents and students need to learn what the ROI is at their college of choice. These are the questions to ask the admissions office:

1. What percentage of recent graduates found a job in his or her chosen field of study?

2. Does the college have any programs with local businesses that hire recent graduates?

3. How many members of your faculty actually work in the fields that they teach? Have they been instrumental in securing jobs in those industries for recent graduates of your institution

4. Does your institution have an established internship or work study program that allows students to get work experience while they are attending school?

5. What is the average student loan debt incurred by your most recent graduates?

No one would buy a home without an engineer's report and many do extensive research before paying for a new or used car. Why should higher education be any different?

I ascertain that by asking the right questions before accepting a college's offer, students and parents are facing the practical reality that a college degree is an investment. It is the institution of higher education's obligation to demonstrate that either a two year or four-year degree is worth the money expended to achieve it.

Parents and students will find that their local community college often offers a better ROI than four-year colleges. It makes sense financially to explore what a local community college offers before committing to spending more than $75,000 for a four-year residential college experience.

Many community colleges now have partnerships with local businesses to train their employees. Others offer certificate programs that fast track a student into a job like court reporting, for example, with starting salaries at around $60,000.

Even if a student wants to receive a four-year degree, it makes financial sense to take the first two years of core courses at a community college and transfer to a four-year institution. Not only are community college courses less expensive than those at four-year institutions, but living at home for two years saves on housing and food costs.

We cannot afford to have our young people saddled with debt before they even begin their careers. It is time for a frank discussion about college affordability, a discussion that should begin long before that admissions letter and financial aid package arrives in the mailbox.

Community college graduates are now earning 15 percent more than liberal arts graduates from a four-year institution.

3 – EMPLOYERS SHOULD VALUE THE TWO-YEAR DEGREE

April 18, 2013

A recent article in *The Chronicle of Higher Education* outlined why employers are disenchanted with recent college graduates. It appears that these graduates lack the ability to think critically, analyze data and communicate effectively. Aren't these all skills that are supposedly the cornerstone of a four-year liberal arts education? In addition, *The Chronicle* goes on to report that companies can no longer afford on-the-job training and expect colleges to provide graduates who are well-prepared to enter the workforce.

Should colleges and universities offer vocational training? Do we need to re-examine how we are preparing students for the workforce of the 21st century? Finally, should a four-year degree be the basic requirement for all jobs?

Years ago, high schools would often have two tracks – one for an academic diploma and the other a vocational degree. Academically inclined students would head off to college while their counterparts in the vocational track would become mechanics, secretaries, electricians and plumbers. In the end, everyone had a well-paying job, bought a home and retired with a pension. That world is gone.

Is it time for us to re-think the higher education career track? As the president of the nation's largest singly-accredited community college system, I am in regular contact with Indiana businesses that are in desperate need of highly trained workers. Without these employees, they would have to outsource work overseas. Why provide a job for someone in Beijing when a resident of South Bend could do it just as well?

But are guidance counselors advising students to get a degree from a community college that would virtually guarantee them a job when they graduate? Or is there still a stigma attached to a community college degree? Shouldn't we give credit to the displaced factory worker who enters college at the age of 50 to be retrained? Or the high school student who would much rather study air conditioning systems over Dante?

The Center on Education in the Workforce at Georgetown University has recognized a new trend. Community college graduates are now earning 15 percent more than liberal arts graduates from a four-year institution. The Center also estimates that 29 million jobs paying middle class wages don't require a bachelor's degree. With a two-year degree, air traffic controllers make $113,547, dental hygienists $70,408, nuclear technicians $68,533 and fashion designers $63, 170 according to Career Builder.com.

Is it time that all employers review job requirements and eliminate the pre-requisite that applicants must have a four-year degree when someone with an associate degree would be equally as qualified?

We are doing our young people a disservice if we expect them to attend a four-year college and not graduate with the training to get a job. This is particularly true if they have more than $25,000 in student loans to re-pay.

Institutions need more internship programs so that students graduate with work experience. They need professors who have real-world experience in their field, not just a list of publications in obscure journals. Finally, they need to re-evaluate how they are teaching problem solving and critical thinking. If employees are looking for these skills, it is our obligation to give students this training.

Let's start by recognizing that someone with a two-year degree may be as equally qualified as a student with a four-year degree. Slamming the door of employment opportunities on someone, simply because he could not afford to attend a four-year institution, defeats the purpose of higher education.

I believe we need to do a better job in understanding the obstacles that community college students face in their desire to have a better life through educational opportunities.

4 – SUPPORTING COMMUNITY COLLEGE STUDENTS

August 26, 2015

Remember college? Four years dedicated to learning. Long nights discussing how to change the world with people who would become your lifelong friends. Sleeping late because your classes started at 10:00 a.m. Professors who encouraged you and advised you on your future. Interesting work/study projects that challenged you.

Now imagine, if while you were in college, you had to support a family and work more than 35 or more hours a week at a low-paying job as a home health aide or fast food worker.

You have to worry about childcare. Overcrowding at your school means that you're shut out of the classes you need for your degree. There is no time to make new friends. Adjunct faculty bring real-time expertise to the classroom, but often don't have office hours. Even parking and getting enough sleep – seemingly everyday concerns – loom large amid the long hours and constant stress.

That's the experience of many of the more than 10.5 million students in this country who attend community colleges. One out of three community college students has family income of less than $20,000, and 69 percent work 35 hours or more a week.

Community colleges are home to non-traditional students – the displaced worker, the returning soldier, the single mom. Often these students need to take remedial courses in English and math before they can even pursue a degree or certificate program. They struggle to manage work, family obligations and studies. This precarious balancing act can often fall apart with a change in their work schedule, a sick child or a broken down car.

I don't want to imply that we should feel sorry for community college students. They don't want our pity. But I believe we need to do a better job in understanding the obstacles that they face in their desire to have a better life through educational opportunities.

Community college students are hardworking and dedicated. Yet those who only crunch the numbers often only see their college completion rates and hold them to the same standards as traditional students, who have the luxury of attending college without worrying about money and have no responsibilities pulling them away from their studies.

Thirty-six percent of community college students are the first in their family to attend college. This means that they lack role models and navigating through a degree program may be more difficult for them.

We need a new formula for calculating the success rate of community college students. If they take six years to get a degree, we should applaud them. When they have to drop out, we should continue to reach out to them and see what can be done to get them to re-enroll. We need to find them apprenticeships with local companies so they can earn while they learn. And when they do get a degree or a complete a certificate program, publish their names and stories in the local newspaper as an inspiration to others.

President Obama's idea of free community college captivated our imagination. In Tennessee with a Republican Governor and in Oregon with a Democrat as Governor this is already happening. We in education will watch closely what transpires in these states. Will more people decide to get a degree if it is free?

I believe as a nation everyone should have access to higher education. To lift people out of poverty, to transform lives, and to show future generations that the American dream is still possible.

Let's stop talking about what community college students are not accomplishing. Let's celebrate each step they make toward fulfilling their dream to becoming a police officer, an EMT, a nurse, a firefighter or a skilled worker in the factories of the future.

Those who get their education at a community college make us stronger as a nation. They deserve our support.

The resource for technical training is often times the local community college, where tuition can be as low as $2,500.

5 – THE CASE FOR CAREER AND TECHNICAL EDUCATION

March 27, 2015

R obert Reich, the distinguished author and Secretary of Labor in the Clinton Administration, recently published an excellent piece on why a four-year college education isn't for everyone.

As the president of Ivy Tech in Indiana, the nation's largest singly-accredited community college system, I couldn't agree more.

High school students around the country are now in a frenzy as they wait for acceptance letters from their college of choice. Many hope to get into prestigious institutions, believing that this will guarantee them a well-paying job upon graduation. To do this, they will accumulate an average of $24,000 in student loans. Those who go to big-name schools will likely owe a lot more.

We need to change our way of thinking about college education. As thousands of recent graduates have discovered, a four-year degree isn't an automatic gateway into the American middle class. Mr. Reich notes that last year the Federal Reserve Bank of New York found that 46 percent of recent college graduates ended up in jobs that didn't require a college degree.

As the former CEO of Delco Remy International, I know firsthand how important it is to have skilled workers. However, because parents continue to view working in a factory as not a viable career option for their children, we are now facing a skills gap in American manufacturing.

The Manufacturing Institute and Deloitte recently issued a report, "The Skills Gap in U.S. Manufacturing 2015 and Beyond," that indicates that the skills gap is widening.

In the next decade, manufacturing will require three and half million new workers as more than 2.7 million baby boomers retire and 700,000 jobs are created through economic expansion. But just 1.4 million of these jobs are expected to be filled, leaving two million good jobs open by the year 2025.

Manufacturing remains a vitally important sector of the economy, as each job creates 2.5 additional jobs for other goods and services, most of them local. The benefits are clear: "For every $1 invested in manufacturing, another $1.37 in additional value is created in other sectors," the Manufacturing Institute/Deloitte report states.

Thus, a new way of thinking about manufacturing jobs needs to get started in this country, and this new thinking must take root in our high schools. Unfortunately, many public high schools don't offer career and technical training that would prepare their graduates for manufacturing jobs. In addition, high school guidance counselors, looking to increase a school's college acceptance rate, don't offer help to a student who may be better suited for a career as a plumber or a welder.

Today, the resource for such training is often times the local community college, where tuition can be as low as $2,500, and much of it will be covered by Pell grants. The return on investment can be very impressive.

America should look to the success of the German apprenticeship program, which offers a dual track of skills training and general education, and to enlightened manufacturers who know the value of a skilled and educated worker.

For example, at Cummins Inc., a global power leader in Indiana that designs, manufactures, sells and services diesel engines and related technology around the world, Ivy Tech has placed over 200 apprentices in various programs while at the same time preparing them in the classroom to receive The Manufacturing Skill Standards Council's Certified Production Technician certification.

This certification addresses the core technical competencies of highly skilled production workers in all sectors of manufacturing. The certificate can be obtained after a year of study and passing a national exam. It is recognized by manufacturers nationwide.

Community colleges have been in the forefront of designing curricula that train workers to benefit the manufacturers in their community. For example, at GE Aviation, Ivy Tech is developing programs to recruit and train employees for a plant scheduled to open in Lafayette. Not infrequently, a corporate decision to open a manufacturing plant in a particular city is contingent upon a partnership with a local community college.

It can't be emphasized enough that we need to change our thinking about manufacturing jobs. Students shouldn't feel that they have failed because they elect not to attend college, but instead, opt to continue their education by getting a manufacturing certificate from a community college. These jobs offer good starting salaries at around $45,000 a year – probably a lot more than a degreed barista is making – as well as lifetime opportunities for advancement.

As Robert Reich so eloquently put it: "America clings to the conceit that four years of college are necessary for everyone and looks down its nose at people who don't have college degrees. This has to stop. Young people need an alternative. That alternative should be a world-class system of vocational-technical education."

It makes good financial sense for a student to take core courses online at a community college and then transfer those credits to a four-year institution.

6 – THE BENEFITS OF ONLINE LEARNING

January 30, 2013

I strongly believe that the future of higher education lies with online learning. Increasingly, colleges and university students now find themselves with other obligations beyond that of getting a degree. Jobs and family commitments make equal demands on their time. Having the option of taking online classes and studying on their own time is critically important. At the same time, many state institutions are unable to accommodate all those who want to take classes on campus, escalating the demand for online learning.

Finally, lifelong learning must now be a part of everyone's career plans. In today's job market, taking online courses helps workers remain competitive and they don't need to take time off from their jobs to do this.

Community colleges have been in the forefront of online learning. In the 2010-11 semester, Ivy Tech in Indiana had more than 79,000 unduplicated students in 300 credit-earning online courses. Governor Jerry Brown of California just announced a pilot program, offering low-cost online courses to the state's public institutions of higher education. The emphasis will be placed on course work for entry-level math, college algebra, and elementary statistics – subjects that normally have high failure rates.

Students need to determine if online learning is an option for them because not everyone does well with this type of study. Some questions that any potential online students should ask are whether or not they can learn independently; how organized they are with their time; whether they are computer savvy; their level of reading comprehension; and if they have at least ten hours a week to devote to each course.

Many make the mistake of assuming that an online class will be easier than one taken in a traditional classroom. Often online instructors assign more reading materials than required in a regular classroom to ensure that students are engaged. Motivation is key to an online student's success as is his ability to reach out to both instructors and fellow students, using software such as Blackboard.

That software program seamlessly integrates social media, making it possible to create online communities that are course specific. Blogs, tweets, podcasts, webcasts, online chats, discussion boards, and virtual study jams are all part of the online mix. Success in an online course often depends on how connected a student feels to his instructor and fellow students.

I believe that online learning has the potential to revolutionize higher education. Students will be able to learn at their own pace and problems as simple as finding a place to park on campus will be eliminated. Public colleges and universities simply cannot build new facilities to accommodate all those who need credits in higher education. In addition, credit hours taken online, particularly at a community college, are often less expensive. It therefore makes good financial sense for a student to take core courses online at a community college and then transfer those credits to a four-year institution.

Local businesses can also benefit from online learning. At Ivy Tech, we work directly with local manufacturing firms to meet their future workforce needs. Online learning not only trains the workers of the future, it can also provide a career path for someone employed, who needs to learn new skills. Employers should recommend online courses that will help with career advancement and, if possible, offer tuition re-imbursement.

For online learning to succeed, it is also essential that we find and train instructors who can adapt to this new medium. Fortunately, new technology makes it possible for instructors to create exciting new ways to learn online that engage students in ways that are more effective than a lecture hall with hundreds of students.

We also need to develop a national transfer pool so that certain online courses can be taken anywhere in the country and then transferred to the student's home institution. No student should face being shut out of a class he needs to get a degree when he can take the same course online at another institution.

Higher education officials need to seek out partnerships with technology companies to ensure that their online learning courses take advantage of all new developments that increase the capacity to learn.

I foresee a time when there will be totally virtual colleges and universities and students will not only take classes at their own institution, but expand their scope by enrolling in courses at the great institutions of learning around the world. Image studying political science with Bill Clinton or science with a Nobel Prize winner.

We are in the early days of online learning. The possibilities are limitless.

COMMUNITY COLLEGES HELP
PEOPLE SUCCEED

Community college changes lives and
supports our society through education and
workforce development. Students are
provided the tools and insight to define and
achieve their goals. Community colleges offer
programs to both launch and build careers in
some of today's most critical fields. Their
affordable tuition allows those who cannot
afford four-year colleges to secure a practical
and valuable education.

It is the responsibility of legislators and educators to do all that we can to help poor students get a college degree.

7 – A BETTER WAY TO HELP LOW-INCOME COLLEGE STUDENTS

January 27, 2013

College attainment is a priority for the Obama Administration, which recognizes that higher education is a proven way to help lift people out of the cycle of poverty. However, in the quest for the country to have more college graduates, we can't penalize students who don't receive a college degree within a certain time period. This is particularly true for community college students, who often take more than two years to receive an Associate degree.

The Pell Grant program is the financial lifeline for poor students. This program is particularly crucial for community college students as it covers tuition costs as well as providing additional money for books, transportation and living expenses.

A recent *New York Times* editorial, "Stop Penalizing Poor College Students," demonstrates how difficult it has become for students at community colleges, which charge by the credit hour, to complete a degree within two years. At private colleges, a Pell Grant often covers the flat amount for one semester of course work. Community colleges charge by the credit hour with an average of $100 per credit.

Pushing all students to register for 15 credit hours as the key to completion might be the right fit for the traditional four-year model, but as the *Times* editorial details, it is not the right approach for community college student.

Not all students are created equal. If a student qualifies for the maximum annual Pell Grant, he would receive $5,645 per year or $2,822.50 each semester. At a community college, this amount would cover 12 credit hours, not the 15 needed to graduate within two years.

In order to take 15 credit hours, a student would need to make up the difference of $705. This is a financial hardship few can afford. In addition, community college students are often older with jobs and family responsibilities and often can't take on a full course load of 15 hours. We are putting a strain on these students who are struggling to balance their finances just well enough to make higher education a priority.

Hawaii instituted "15 to Finish" in 2012 and found that it increased the percentage of students taking 15 credits. However, the most significant improvement was found at universities with flat rate tuition rather than at community colleges that charge by credit hour.

At Indiana's Ivy Tech Community College, its Associated Accelerated Program (ASAP) was recently featured in a *Wall Street Journal* article "College Makes Studying Pay." This program enables students to complete an Associate degree in one year. It provides funding for essentials such as bus fare. The program's completion rate is high – more than 70 percent. Students are recruited from local high schools and asked to commit to living at home and not working during the week while they are in school.

I believe this Ivy Tech program works because we have alleviated a significant financial burden many students face when they decide to attend school. This enables them to focus full-time on their studies. We were fortunate to have funding from the Lumina Foundation that provided $2.3 million to launch the program in 2010.

But we recognize that a program of this nature doesn't work for all community college students. In the case of Ivy Tech, the ASAP program was set up to help recent high school graduates who don't have other commitments on their time or financial resources.

We need to make it easier for community college students to enroll and get a degree by making sure that whether they enroll for twelve credit hours or fifteen that a Pell Grant will provide a financial safety net covering most of their expenses.

What Congress needs to do is re-define full time enrollment and give students who enroll at community colleges a larger Pell Grant if they take more than 12 credit hours. It is the responsibility of legislators and educators to do all that we can to help poor students get a college degree.

Community colleges can fast track a vet into a new career in a matter of months.

8 – COMMUNITY COLLEGE AND RETURNING VETS

April 3, 2013

As the war in Afghanistan winds down, thousands of servicemen and women will return home to a country that is still in the early stages of economic recovery. Helping these warriors transition to civilian life needs to be our number-one priority.

Community colleges have a long history of working with vets. This assistance goes well beyond merely processing the paperwork to get them their educational benefits under the Post-9/11 GI Bill.

Many community colleges operate an office of veterans' affairs that provide everything from career counseling and resume writing to access to local businesses for job placement. Tuition discounts, tuition without residency requirements and fee-waived applications are other important benefits instituted by community colleges on behalf of vets.

Because tuition at these schools is lower than at four-year institutions, vets often have 100 percent of their educational expenses covered. In some cases, they also receive stipends for housing and books. Since the average age of a vet attending community colleges is 25, these schools also have extensive experience working with non-traditional students.

Providing these services have earned many community colleges the designation of being "military friendly" by *GI Jobs* magazine, a free publication that is distributed on military bases.

Dan Fazio, Managing Editor of *GI Jobs* noted:

> Vets gravitate to community colleges because of the variety of educational opportunities they offer. To make up for lost times, some vets may not want an Associate or bachelor's degree and opt instead for a certificate program that enables them to pursue careers as a plumber, EMT technician, electrician, welder or machinist. Community colleges can fast track a vet into a new career in a matter of months.

At Ivy Tech in Indiana, we believe that helping veterans is an important part of our mission to provide seamless access to educational attainment. We are proud to be designated a "military friendly" school.

There are more than 5,000 vets currently enrolled at Ivy Tech. Vets need someone to guide them through the maze of VA benefits. They are accustomed to having structure in their lives and look to institutions like ours to provide it. Ivy Tech has a group of people dedicated to helping them, including a Central Administration VA liaison.

When our vets return home, they want to re-acclimatize themselves with their family and friends rather than pack up and move to another city to go to school. Community colleges are a vital resource. That is why it is so critically important in the months ahead that community colleges increase their outreach to vets and make sure that these brave men and women get the education they need and the jobs they deserve.

Most students 50 and over welcome an opportunity to learn a new skill as they envision themselves as part of the workforce for another 15 to 20 years.

9 – BACK TO COLLEGE AT 50

February 7, 2013

G oing back to school at 50 can be daunting. However, The American Association of Community College Plus 50 Encore Program has set a target of enrolling more than 10,000 students age 50 and older at more than 100 community college campuses. Forty percent of the group will be targeted to earn college credentials by 2015. In 2009, adults age 55 and older made up nearly a fifth of the nation's labor force, the highest share since 1948 when the Bureau of Labor Statistics began tracking age-specific participation rates.

Unemployed older workers face formidable challenges. In 2009 only about 15 percent of them found jobs each month. Many of these older workers have not been in a classroom for more than 30 years. Those still working full-time often also shoulder family responsibilities. But they know that in order to remain competitive in today's job market, they need to sharpen their skills.

Those who find themselves unemployed must learn new skills in order to pursue a different occupation. There is a genuine need in many local communities for workers in the high-demand, high-growth sectors of healthcare, education and social services. These fields are especially appealing to many baby boomers because they provide an opportunity to give back to their community while earning a good salary. Some of these jobs require a two-year degree, but many only require completion of a certificate program. An independent evaluation of the Plus 50 Encore Program found that 89 percent of students agreed that college work-force training helped them acquire new job skills. In fact, 72 percent attributed landing a job to this training. Community colleges are particularly well-positioned to train older workers because they offer a supportive environment, flexible schedules, emphasis on practical job training, and affordable tuition rates.

Many community colleges, such as Ivy Tech in Indiana, already have programs in place with local businesses to provide specific training for their present and future workers. Currently, the Ivy Tech-Northwest Health Industry Institute for Education and Training Services is recruiting 50 plus workers for its Community Health Worker program. Graduates of this program provide health outreach, assistance, and management of the overall health outcomes of patients.

As the healthcare sector evolves under President Obama's new insurance initiatives, these workers will help patients or potential patients receive immediate care before they need to be admitted to a hospital or long-term health setting. This reduces medical costs and is essential to community health. Most students 50 and over welcome an opportunity to learn a new skill as they envision themselves as part of the workforce for another 15 to 20 years. The AACC Plus 50 Encore Completion Program makes it much easier for them to continue contributing to society.

More than 60 percent of all community college students are age 22 or older. On every campus, you will find someone whose story is similar to yours.

10 – COMMUNITY COLLEGES WELCOME CAREER CHANGERS

December 6, 2012

Millions of Americans are unemployed because their jobs have been outsourced overseas. Others are realizing that they need to acquire more advanced skills to stay competitive. Many jobs lost during the recession will never come back. Faced with the prospect of changing careers, many Americans turn to their local community college.

Community colleges are uniquely positioned to help people looking to change careers. These institutions recognize that career changers confront different obstacles to getting a degree than the average student fresh out of high school.

Older students often have family and job responsibilities. Many, having not set foot in a classroom for more than 20 years, are afraid that they aren't ready to pursue a degree or a certification program.

My advice to career changers is to view their local community college as an invaluable partner in their search for a new career. Here are some simple steps they can take:

• Learn to manage your time efficiently. Four to six months before enrolling at a community college, determine how much time you can allot to studying, particularly if you are still working while in school. Changing careers in a big step that will impact every part of your life. Be realistic about how many hours of course work you can manage.

• Don't procrastinate. Visit the campus; talk to an academic advisor; brush up on your computer and Internet skills; and research what businesses are hiring in your area. Are there local companies that have a program with your community college? Ask about the job placement rate for a field of study that interests you.

• Check if there is a U.S. Department of Education Educational Opportunity Center (EOC) in your area and take full advantage of the range of services it provides.

• Research what financial aid is available by searching online under adult community college scholarships. You may be surprised to learn that scholarships are available for students from a minority background or a first generation college student.

• Choose a career path that interests you. Not everyone is cut out to be a nurse or a computer programmer. There are dozens of Associate degrees and certificate programs that lead to well-paying jobs.

• Be prepared to take a placement test, which will determine whether you are ready for college-level material. Your community college website will have material related to its placement test, including a sample test with reading, writing and math sections. Familiarize yourself with this test before you take it, especially if you have not taken a standardized test for many years.

The most important thing to remember is that you are not alone. More than 60 percent of all community college students are age 22 or older. On every campus, you will find someone whose story is similar to yours.

Losing a job can be painful. Preparing for a new career can be daunting. That said, you can rely on your local community college for invaluable guidance every step of the way.

Community colleges are tailoring their programs to regional economies and industries in order to graduate students who can step right in, contribute to economic growth, and make a good living.

11 – PROFESSIONAL CERTIFICATION FROM A COMMUNITY COLLEGE:

A SOLUTION FOR THE UNEMPLOYED

October 31, 2012

While unemployment is now 7.8 percent, the fact remains that there are still more than nine million people jobless – and millions more under-employed. The key to getting people back to work is education and re-training – and this is where community colleges excel.

Older workers with family responsibilities and reduced income don't have the luxury of going back to college full-time to acquire new, marketable skills. That's why certification programs at community colleges are the ideal solution. These programs fast-track workers into a new career usually in less than a year and often for as little as $2,000 in tuition.

Many community colleges certification programs have been set up in conjunction with local businesses. Community colleges are tailoring their programs to regional economies and industries in order to graduate students who can step right in, contribute to economic growth, and make a good living. The manufacturing sector, for example, increasingly needs highly skilled workers and often works in partnership with a community college to provide the required training.

The most popular certificate programs prepare student for jobs in health care, manufacturing, business and technology. At Ivy Tech Community College in Indiana, for instance, there are more than 50 certification programs, providing training in welding, EMS, medical billing and solar instillation, among others. Like many community colleges, Ivy Tech provides customized class schedules for its certification programs that take into account the demands older students face, such as childcare.

What should one look for in a certification program? First, determine if the program was set up to address the existing need of a local corporation to train workers to fill current open job positions. If there are wind turbines in your area, chances are the local community college will offer a certificate for repairing them. That's the case with

Mitchell Technical Institute in South Dakota that offers a one-year certificate qualifying students for work in this field.

Equally important is how well students from a particular community college perform on industry or state-wide certification tests. A low pass rate indicates that the program isn't rigorous enough to enable one to complete for job openings. Alvin College outside of Houston, for example, excels in preparing students in its two-year court reporter certification program with an 80 percent pass rate for the national licensing exam. A court reporter can earn an average of $60,000 a year.

Good certification programs also place students in the field as interns or apprentices for on-the-job training. At South Dakota's Lake Area Technical Institute, future airplane mechanics work on a FedEx jet recently retired from service.

The ultimate test of a certificate program is how many students get jobs in their chosen field. Applicants should search out programs that have job placement rates of at least 75 percent.

The fact remains that many displaced workers will never find another job in their field because technology and global competition have eliminated or outsourced those jobs permanently. These workers have to be open-minded about re-training and certification programs at community colleges that now offer one of the best and fastest paths to employment.

12 – MENTORING CULTIVATES COLLEGE SUCCESS

December 2, 2015

Community college students, who are the first in their family to attend college and from lower income backgrounds, typically struggle in their first year of school. Issues such as balancing family obligations and work issues, along with learning time management and problem solving, often leave them feeling vulnerable and alone.

Research shows that the best way to address this is to pair them with a mentor who can help them navigate through the pitfalls of higher education.

A recent study by the Indiana Commission of Higher Education showed that at Ivy Tech Community College, 45.7 percent of freshmen, who worked with mentors, were retained to their second year. This is an 8.8 percentage point increase about the three-year historical average.

Indiana Commissioner of Higher Education Teresa Lubbers said: "Proactive approaches like this mentoring program ensure our students are never anonymous on campus and that they have the support they need to succeed."

Around the country, other community colleges are reporting unprecedented success with mentorship programs. Hostos Community College in The Bronx, New York, believes its program helps "...students (to) feel supported by college personnel, comfortable and safe in a welcoming environment, and challenged and rewarded by successfully navigating the college process." Mentors strive to help mentees establish "a stronger sense of self-esteem and confidence as they continue their pursuit for enhanced knowledge and higher education."

Research has proven that students, who are connected to and feel comfortable at an institution of higher learning, are more likely to graduate from that institution, as opposed to students who must rely on their own support networks, who are more likely to transfer or drop-out.

Other community colleges join forces with on-campus groups such as Scottsdale Community College in Arizona, which works closely with the campus Women's Leadership Group, as well as an innovative initiative that pairs armed forces veterans incoming as students with veterans already enrolled. The mentors show the student vets how to adjust to campus life, identify on-and off-campus resources, and gain invaluable advice on how to balance school, work and family life.

Roxbury Community College, outside of Boston, trains mentors to help younger students, ages 18-24, clarify academic goals and develop a plan to reach them. The program also assists them with access to the school's resources such as financial aid. There are even mentee/mentor group activities and events.

At Westchester Community College, faculty members volunteer to mentor students through scheduled meetings where they can discuss their academic needs, share their goals and address any concerns.

Whether it is someone fresh from high school, a veteran, or an older student returning to school for the first time in 20 years, mentoring programs have proven to be invaluable for academic success. These programs can be challenging to implement because they require a commitment of time by the mentors, who in some instances are faculty already stretched to their limits with classes.

However, mentoring programs work, and community colleges should do whatever it takes to offer them to all students. It is a proven path to success.

It is imperative that states take on this initiative with their own resources, as it could take years for the federal government to fund free community college.

13 – A BLUEPRINT FOR FREE COMMUNITY COLLEGE

Every governor and community college president in the country is paying close attention to Tennessee's successful free community college program. The hope is that if this can be accomplished in Tennessee, there is no reason why it can't happen nationwide.

Republican Governor Bill Haslam instituted Tennessee Promise in February 2014, making the state the first in the nation to provide free community college. The Obama Administration saw Tennessee Promise as a model that could work across the country and advocated free community college for all in January of 2015.

Governor Haslam realized how important a community college education is after traveling the state on a listening tour and asking business and industry leaders what they needed to build their workforce. What he learned was that vacancies in many industries were not being filled due to a lack of qualified workers, particularly in IT and information systems. These jobs required a post-secondary education and qualifications that the state's 13 community colleges and 27 colleges of applied technology could readily provide.

As the former CEO of a manufacturing company, I know first-hand that companies in Indiana are facing the same shortage of workers. Ivy Tech now works with hundreds of Indiana businesses to train their future workforce. Many of our students already attend Ivy Tech for free because they are enrolled in an apprenticeship program where their employer pays their tuition and they earn while they learn.

The board of College Promise, advocating "free community college for responsible students," was formed to move the idea of free community college forward. The board recently met in Tennessee to learn more about the successful practices instituted by that state. The national Advisory Board is a separate initiative under Civic Nation, a non-partisan, 501(c)(3), non-profit organization led by Martha J. Kanter, a former U.S. Under Secretary of Education.

As a board member of College Promise, I am impressed by Tennessee's initiatives. The state starts preparing students for community college while they are in high school by working with guidance counselors and letting every student know that community college is free.

At the present time, Tennessee Promise is only for students graduating high school. The state simply does not have the resources to enroll non-traditional students. High school students, who graduated in 2015, marked the first class to have free community college.

This number of students enrolled at Tennessee's community colleges has risen dramatically. There are now 16,291 students enrolled, representing a 24.7 percent increase at community colleges and 20 percent at colleges of applied technology – formerly known as technical schools.

Tennessee has initiated a Summer Bridge Program that helps high school students, who have enrolled in community college, become more college-ready, both academically and socially.

All of these students are assigned to a volunteer mentor – often a business person from their community who can guide them through the community college admission process. There are 9,301 mentors in Tennessee.

The state is removing any financial obstacles, particularly for students who would be the first in the family to attend college and have no guidance on how to get financial aid, or students from low-income families.

In 2015, Tennessee became the highest-rated state in the country for the percentage of high school seniors who completed the Free Application for Federal Student Aid (FAFSA). This is vitally important. Many low-income students already receive enough aid so that their community college tuition is free. But they have no way of knowing this unless they fill out FAFSA.

In addition, Tennessee has instituted the "last-dollar" scholarship. This works by factoring in what a student's financial aid package would be after receiving a Pell Grant and a Tennessee Hope scholarship, which is based on merit. The state fills in the last-dollar gap, which averages around $970 per student.

An interesting component of Tennessee Promise is the requirement that every student do eight hours of community service. The architects of the plan believed that this would establish a powerful connection between the student and where he studies that would be mutually beneficial.

Students are required to begin their postsecondary education in the Fall, directly following high school graduation and remain at an eligible institution for four consecutive semesters. They must enroll full time each semester and maintain satisfactory academic progress, which at most institutions is the equivalent of earning a 2.0 GPA each semester.

My College Promise colleagues were most interested in how Tennessee expects to pay for free community college. The funding comes from $110 million from the state's lottery reserves along with a $47 million endowment, created by the state General Assembly. I think it is imperative that states take on this initiative with their own resources, as it could take years for the federal government, despite President Obama's good intentions, to fund free community college.

Tennessee has shown that free community college is possible. It is now up to community college presidents to find ways to work with their own state governments to make community college free in their own communities to local high school students. I believe that this will be a true game-changer in higher education.

For retirees, community colleges offer an opportunity to stay mentally and physically active, and at a price that's hard to pass up.

14 – RETIREES RETURN TO COMMUNITY COLLEGE

January 5, 2016

I n addition to seeking a warmer climate, lower taxes and housing costs, many retirees are relocating to college towns that provide intellectual simulation for their golden years.

Many community colleges court these seniors with free or low-cost tuition. According to the American Association of Community Colleges, about 84 percent of its members offer courses specifically for students 50 and older. The cost of tuition is very affordable, averaging less than $2,500 a year for a full-time community college student. Community colleges also promote online courses for seniors who are not able to travel to a campus or want to save money on gas and parking fees.

Often, community colleges also provide non-degree programs in arts such as ceramics, jewelry, drawing, painting, etc., while some offer cooking courses, piano lessons, yoga classes and water aerobics.

Terra State Community College in Fremont, Ohio, offers those 60 and over the opportunity to enroll tuition-free in any course. A senior can take anything from a "History of Rock and Roll" course to creative writing. In addition, the school has a Life Scholars program for those over the age of 50, which offers travel opportunities and special seminars.

Paradise Valley Community College in Phoenix, Arizona, offers a range of fitness programs designed for senior students. Its Silver Sneakers Fitness Program is covered by many health plans such as AARP Medicare Supplement Insurance. There are classes in Zumba Gold and Tai Chi for seniors, as well as senior-themed parties offered in its spacious fitness center.

Eastern Iowa Community College in Davenport recognizes that many seniors want to become more technically savvy to connect with grandchildren through email, Facebook and Skype, as well as to take advantage of online shopping and researching locales for future trips. Its low-cost computer courses range from an overview of Microsoft Office for $34 to learning how to navigate the Internet for $29. The school also offers yoga classes and a comprehensive exercise course, combining stretching, weight training and low-impact cardio workout.

Ivy Tech in Indiana as well offers seniors the opportunity to attend classes free of charge. As with other community colleges, there is a small fee for signing up and students are responsible for purchasing books.

Perhaps the best argument to be made for attending a community college as a retiree is that these institutions are accustomed to working with older students, and a 60-plus student will feel right at home in a setting where many of their classmates are over 50.

Ongoing educational opportunities and service to the local community are what set community colleges apart from other institutions of higher learning. For retirees, community colleges offer an opportunity to stay mentally and physically active, and at a price that's hard to pass up.

HELPING AMERICA'S EMPLOYERS

Business calls it the "skills gap," and it is a major problem for both employers and our economy. Community colleges across the country address this need for people highly trained in technology, manufacturing, allied medical professions and many more fields in close collaboration with local companies to close the gap.

Clearly, Aviation Technology is a growing field and community colleges are a major source of skilled workers for the industry.

15 – THE BOOMING FIELD OF AVIATION TECHNOLOGY

June 6, 2013

The U.S. Department of Labor estimates that by 2014 nearly 40 percent of employees in large aviation and aerospace businesses will be eligible for retirement, creating a huge demand for trained technicians in the field. Initially, the sector will grow by 6 percent for aircraft equipment mechanics and technicians, who perform scheduled maintenance on airplanes and helicopters.

Median annual pay for someone with an Associate degree in Airframe Maintenance or Powerplant, who passes the Federal Aviation Administration (FAA) mechanics certificate exams, was $53,280 in 2010. Graduates work with airlines, cargo fleets, airline manufacturers, helicopter operators and corporate aircraft fleets. They perform maintenance on airplanes and helicopters as well as conducting inspections required by the FAA.

Clearly, Aviation Technology is a growing field and community colleges are a major source of skilled workers for the industry. And it's not just planes. Wind turbines, some race cars and even boats are powered by turbine engines similar to those on aircraft, opening up additional job possibilities for trained technicians.

At Ivy Tech community college in Indiana, there has been an increase in enrollment in our Northeast Aviation Technology Program located at Smith Field Airport in Fort Wayne. The new $2.3 million Aviation Center has attracted 82 students with capacity for 200. The school works closely with area businesses such as Pinnacle Airlines and AAR, who recruit aviation graduates. The course of instruction covers control methods, team building, technical writing, and computer skills. Tuition including labs is around $3,300 a year.

In addition, Ivy Tech has set up a program that has enrolled 23 high school students interested in this exciting field. Those students are prepared to take the FAA exam for Powerplant certification with the option of returning after graduation to complete the Airframe License classes or work toward an Associate of Applied Science in Aviation Maintenance Technology.

A $1.5 million aviation maintenance grant from the U.S. Department of Labor, earmarked to help displaced workers in Northeast Indiana, has enabled Ivy Tech to train sheet metal installers, airframe installers and electrical installers – all skills needed by local businesses.

Elsewhere, South Seattle Community College works closely with Boeing to meet its workforce needs. The school has a long history of producing aviation technicians, dating back to the 1930s when it was Edison Technical College. Aircraft mechanics in the Seattle area with just a two year Associate degree and certification earn more than $78,000.

Portland Community College in Oregon has trained aviation mechanics since 1969. The institution operates a 30,000 square-foot, two-hanger complex with 16 aircraft, used exclusively for instruction, including helicopters that are often used in law enforcement.

Before recommending a four-year college, high school guidance counselors and parents should determine whether a student would be better served at a community college in a program that virtually guarantees employment. The same is true for returning vets and displaced workers. Aviation technology is one of these fields.

*Community colleges are on the front lines
educating future police officers, firefighters,
private investigators, forensic science technicians,
crime scene investigators and correction officers.*

16 – CRIMINAL JUSTICE AND COMMUNITY COLLEGE

July 4, 2013

The field of criminal justice is expanding rapidly. The Bureau of Labor Statistics says it will increase by 10 percent through 2018. Television shows such as *CSI, Law & Order* and *NCIS* have introduced millions to the world of crime fighting. This new interest, combined with a growing prison population and increased dependence on law enforcement stemming from terrorist threats, means many criminal justice jobs now require more than a high school diploma.

Community colleges are on the front lines, educating future police officers, firefighters, private investigators, forensic science technicians, crime scene investigators and correction officers. While some of these jobs may only require a high school diploma or GED, employers now give preference to applicants with military experience or an Associate degree in criminal justice. There is also an increased demand for paralegals. Medium starting salaries for these occupations are between $40,000 and $50,000 per year according to the Department of Labor.

In addition, individuals who want to pursue a career with the FBI, Homeland Security, and Department of Justice or as criminologists, probation officer or INS agent, for example, will need to get a BS degree. Many of these students start their education at a community college because it is less expensive than initially enrolling in a four-year institution as a freshman.

At Ivy Tech in Indiana, we are fortunate to have Dr. Richard Weinblatt, a former police chief and expert in the field of criminal justice, as our Dean of the School of Public and Social Services and the School of Education. Dr. Weinblatt believes that higher education is essential in the field of criminal justice. "In the classroom, students study with others from various backgrounds such as race, gender, and sexual orientation. This experience enables them to be more open minded and helps with their communication skills, which is vital to a successful career in criminal justice," Dr. Weinblatt notes.

Other community colleges around the country now have exemplary programs to train first responders. Oakland Community College in Michigan created The Combined Regional Emergency Services Training Center in cooperation with local police, fire and EMS agencies. This training "city" provides realistic settings for real-life problems faced by emergency responders.

Elsewhere, Waubonsee Community College in Illinois provides students with their own CSI laboratory. Portland Community College in Oregon has a continuing education and training program for criminal justice professionals already working in the field.

Criminal justice is a fascinating field, one that offers many opportunities for advancement through both state and federal exams. Many states recognize the critical role that community colleges currently play in educating those committed public servants, who protect our local communities, by providing increased financial support. A degree in criminal justice from a community college trains individuals who can both help those in trouble with the law as well as protect our communities.

Culinary schools charge around $19,000 for a certification program and around $37,000 for a two-year degree. The same two year Associate degree at a community college would cost less than $10,000.

17 – THE HOSPITALITY INDUSTRY AND COMMUNITY COLLEGE

May 16, 2013

The last couple of years have seen the rise of celebrity chefs as top television personalities. Programs like *Chopped, Top Chef, Cupcake Wars* and *Master Chef* have introduced millions to the fast-paced life of the kitchen. Working as a chef was once viewed as a dreary job in the service industry. It is now viewed as a respected and well-paid position. Chefs are the new rock stars.

Starting out, a chef can earn $18 to $20 an hour with an opportunity for advancement. The hospitality sector remains strong and is positioned for additional growth over the next several years.

Community colleges recognized that they could train future chefs for less money than schools of culinary arts.

These culinary schools charge around $19,000 for a certification program and around $37,000 for a two-year degree. The same two year Associate degree at a community college like Ivy Tech in Indiana would cost less than $10,000. Ivy Tech is now "the largest provider of post-secondary undergraduate hospitality studies" in the state.

In addition to chefs, the hospitality industry employs meeting planners, convention center coordinators, beverage managers, dietary managers and restaurant administrators. Many of these jobs only require certificates that can be obtained after a sequence of technical and professional courses and passing a national exam. Jobs in these fields pay anywhere from $30,000 to $60,000 and offer opportunity for growth.

States not usually thought of as tourist destinations are earmarking more money to attract tourists. Michigan, for example, has seen a dramatic rise in tourism following its successful television campaign "Pure Michigan." Tourist dollars, in turn, support more jobs in the hospitality industry. The U.S. Department of Labor projects 16 percent growth in this sector compared to 14 percent growth in all industries combined.

Young people have traditionally made up most of the workforce for the hospitality sector. This is slowly changing as more older workers and those displaced from manufacturing jobs, for example, are being recruited. The image of the industry is also changing largely due to channels like the Food Network, which depicts jobs in restaurants and hotels as challenging and rewarding.

Individuals interested in exploring certification or an Associate degree in hospitality should check with their local community college to find out about partnerships local businesses may already have in place to train their workforce.

Has your city just increased the size of its convention center? Are there more restaurants springing up in one section of town? Are there new assisted-living centers? If so, it's a safe bet that there will be the need for more hospitality workers. It is also an industry that provides professional development and promotes from within, which is important to those who want a career rather than just a job.

Community colleges are in the vanguard of insuring that well-paying manufacturing jobs are not shipped overseas but stay in the community.

18 – COMMUNITY COLLEGES AND THE MANUFACTURING SECTOR

December 12, 2013

For decades the manufacturing sector provided jobs with good wages. Today, however, the Manufacturing Institute states that 82 percent of manufacturers report a moderate or serious skills gap in skilled production, and 74 percent of manufacturers report that the skills gap has hurt their company's ability to expand operations.

But what is most alarming is that an estimated 2.7 million U.S. manufacturing employees, nearly a fourth of the total, are 55 or over. According to a 2010 article in The Financial Times, 40 percent of Boeing workers, and nearly half of Rockwell Collins' workers will be eligible for retirement by 2016. We cannot afford to have these jobs shipped overseas because we don't have the skilled workers to fill them.

The Manufacturing Institute was one of the first organizations to address the lack of skilled workers. The Institute launched the NAM-Endorsed Skills Certification System to address the skills gap challenge and to promote a renaissance of manufacturing education across the country. What this system does is provide a set of the industry-recognized credentials that workers need to be successful in entry-level positions in any manufacturing environment.

Community colleges were among the first to embrace these new standards by creating certification programs that train students for jobs as varied as the manufacturing of orthopedic devices to repairing wind turbines. Local manufacturers began reaching out to community colleges asking them to train their future workforce. Often these students were displaced workers or had lost their jobs through outsourcing. This cohort, many over the age of 50, presented a new challenge - how to train students who hadn't been a classroom for more than 20 years.

Partnerships between community colleges and manufacturing companies have been remarkably successful largely because they have been in the forefront of providing customized training that leads directly to a well-paying job.

For example, Siemens developed the Design Technology Program associate degree at Iowa Western Community College, providing students with the skills to "effectively translate ideas from inventors, engineers, planner and designers into visual graphic form."

Connecticut Community College's College of Technology developed the Regional Center for Next Generation Manufacturing, which places educators with advanced manufacturing companies for 4 week externships. These instructors received hands-on training that they then brought back to the classroom.

When St. Louis lost 10,000 jobs in the auto industry, St. Louis Community College offered training in new technologies that enabled many of the displaced workers to get jobs at Boeing assembling jets.

Northeast Wisconsin Technical College worked with the North Coast Marine Manufacturing Alliance to train skilled workers capable of producing the best ships in the world. One of the member companies was awarded a contract to build 10 Littoral Combat ships for the U.S. Navy. This contract created 1,000 new jobs, jobs that might not have come to Wisconsin if there weren't trained workers waiting to fill them.

As the former CEO of Delco Remy International, a manufacturing company, I know first hand how vital it is to have a highly-skilled workforce. Indiana is a leader in manufacturing, and Ivy Tech, its community college system, works closely with corporations like Cummins to ensure we are providing our students with the training they need to fill jobs in the manufacturing sector. These jobs pay an average of $45,000 a year and offer opportunity for advancement.

In January, we will launch a unique academic-industry-blended 75 hour co-op Advanced Manufacturing degree program. Our students will gain valuable on-the-job experience with some of Indiana's top manufacturing and logistics companies, working as interns two days a week. Upon graduation, they will have received training in the most current and relevant industry technology as well as having real world experience. Our goal is to have them work for the companies where they interned.

Through the generosity of Alcoa Foundation, we also recently launched "Get Skills to Work," a program that provides free manufacturing training for veterans. Graduates will receive interviews with area manufacturers through the Tri-State Manufacturers' Alliance. The Get-Skills-to-Work coalition includes more than 500 manufacturers and focuses on training for veterans, translating the skills they learned in the military into manufacturing careers.

Flexibility, vision and commitment are all-important factors in working with the nation's manufacturers. Community colleges are in the vanguard of insuring that well-paying manufacturing jobs are not shipped overseas but stay in the community.

The associate degree is without question the most affordable pathway to a nursing career.

19 – A THREAT TO THE BACKBONE OF OUR HEALTHCARE SYSTEM: RESTRICTING ACCESS TO NURSING

November 16, 2013

While visiting a friend in the hospital, I was immediately impressed with the quality of care he received from nurses. They were his lifeline and largely responsible for his complete recovery.

Nurses are the backbone of our nation's healthcare system. As our population ages, the continued growth of our nursing workforce will be more critical than ever before.

Despite this fact, a burgeoning movement is underway that would limit access to careers in the field. A small contingent of special interest groups is advocating that certain hospitals – those seeking to attain "nursing magnet" status – restrict employment only to those with bachelor's degrees in nursing (BSN). Their efforts would have catastrophic results not just for those with associate degrees in nursing (ASN), but for our nation's healthcare system as a whole. It may also result in increased healthcare costs.

One of my greatest concerns is that their position is supported by claims that just aren't true. For example, those promoting the BSN as a necessary prerequisite to a nursing career imply that ASN-credentialed nurses provide a diminished quality of care as compared to BSN-credentialed nurses. However, there is no evidence supporting these claims. Even studies that call for an increase in BSN-credentialed nurses – including a 2010 study by the Institute of Medicine of the National Academies – have found no relationship between the education level and patient outcomes.

The primary reason that a different credential is not correlated with a different patient outcome is: all candidates, regardless of their education level, take the same national licensure exam to become RNs – the National Certification Licensing Examination (NCLEX). Today, in fact, the majority of new RNs are educated in ASN programs. If the NCLEX is the true determinant of career readiness, then, how can it be argued that one path that prepares students for the NCLEX is superior to another? The truth is, this argument is invalid, and it obscures the very real need for nursing candidates to have options.

For many, a BSN is the best choice because it gives them an advantage in competing for management positions. For others, even a BSN is not enough: if they want a career in nursing education, they will likely need to attain a master's of science in nursing (MSN). For others, however, an ASN is not only the best choice – it may be the only choice, given the unparalleled affordability offered by community colleges.

This is certainly the case for nursing candidates who chose Ivy Tech Community College. Our full-time students pay just $3,334 per year for tuition, a fraction of the cost of the average Indiana college. It's notable, too, that this does not factor in fees, room, and board charged by other colleges, which in itself adds up to thousands of dollars. This helps students and their families stay out of debt and make it more likely that they will remain in college since they are less likely to be held back due to competing financial responsibilities. The ASN is without question the most affordable pathway to a nursing career. Retaining that option will make the profession accessible to the largest number of aspiring nurses. Why should we cause more debt for some that are already in a difficult financial position, who are looking to find a career that can change that?

The ASN credential plays another critical role in preparing professionals in that credits earned in the program can be transferred to four-year institutions. So for some that means if they wish to pursue a BSN they can get started at a community college, continue on toward a BSN, and save thousands of dollars in the process. The bottom line is that nurses are the backbone of our healthcare system, and we will need more of them – a projected 1 million additional RNs by 2018 – as our population ages. Our best chance of ensuring that we are prepared to respond to this need is by making the profession accessible to all qualified candidates, including those credentialed with an ASN or a BSN.

So, when you hear the arguments in favor of limiting the nursing profession to those with a BSN, ask yourself whether such restrictions would be in the best interest of everyone who depends upon our healthcare system, or just those who would benefit from shutting out otherwise qualified candidates.

In many cases, a student with a certificate in information technology will probably earn more than the art history major over a lifetime of employment.

20 – COMMUNITY COLLEGES AND TECH SUPPORT

June 17, 2015

Whether it is a Mom-and-Pop business or a multi-national company, they both share a common need – reliable tech support. But we are facing a crisis in this country because there are more jobs available in technology than there are highly skilled people to fill them. If America is to remain competitive, I believe the answer lies with the work of community colleges.

The field of tech support has exploded over the past 10 years. The Bureau of Labor Statistics projects that jobs in computer system design and tech support will grow 49 percent from 2012 to 2022. As companies look to upgrade their existing systems, there will be further demand for highly skilled IT workers. Salaries start at $60,000 a year with tremendous opportunities for growth.

The best news is that one doesn't need a bachelor degree or, in some cases, even an associate degree to find employment in systems operations.

Community colleges offer many certificate programs that prepare one for a well-paying job in tech support. These certificates are nationally recognized and often can be obtained in less than two years. Many community colleges offer these certificate programs online.

Once a student completes a certificate and finds a job, many enroll again to update their skills or work toward an associate degree. Some proactive employers will pay for their workers to take these courses.

Microsoft and Cisco are among the companies that have established their own certificate programs at community colleges so that students will be trained to work with their operating systems anywhere in the country.

If community colleges do a good job in training students for help desk/technical support, American companies will find it more advantageous to keep these jobs in the United States and not ship them overseas – or import workers from overseas to fill them.

Another computer-related field with great growth is cyber security. This is of tantamount importance to a company, which today must do everything possible to keep its proprietary and customer data safe. This field only requires a certificate in Cyber Security/Information Assurance to get a job.

A web development certificate provides one with the skills to create and maintain a website. And Database management and administration skills are critical to any business; employers are hiring individuals with certificates in this area.

At Ivy Tech, we offer these certificate programs in the daytime, evenings and on weekends to serve our students because we know from experience that those who take these courses find well-paying jobs. Extensive hands-on training is provided in our computer and network labs. We also seek out apprenticeships at local companies providing our students with invaluable on-the-job training.

Just recently, we announced a public-private collaboration with the National Institute for Metalworking Skills and Lightweight Innovations for Tomorrow. There are nearly 39,000 job openings in Indiana, Kentucky, Michigan, Ohio and Tennessee and, we will help train these workers. We plan to have the first-ever industry standards for educating and training the industrial technology maintenance workforce.

We need to change the way we think about higher education in this country. Not all students have the luxury of studying art history at a four-year liberal arts colleges. High school guidance counselors and parents should determine if a student would benefit from enrolling in a certificate program that would enable them to get a good job in systems operations in less than two years.

In many cases, a student with a certificate in information technology will probably earn more than the art history major over a lifetime of employment.

Community colleges are on the front lines in training America's healthcare professionals, and will continue to serve our growing healthcare needs.

21 – COMMUNITY COLLEGES AND HEALTHCARE

July 1, 2015

The Bureau of Labor Statistics estimates that the healthcare sector will add the most new jobs between 2012 and 2022. Even before the Affordable Care Act was passed, the healthcare sector represented nearly 19 percent of all spending in the nation's economy and 13 percent of all jobs. Community colleges are the pipeline for training and certifying more than half of all healthcare workers.

With more Americans getting healthcare coverage through the ACA, and with baby boomers getting older and inevitably experiencing more issues with their health, there is an increased need for RNs, LPNs, medical assistants, dental hygienists, EMTs, paramedics and pharmacy technicians. These jobs require either an associate degree or certification.

In a 2011 report, "Creating Opportunities in Health Care: The Community College Role in Workforce Partnership," the authors point out that community colleges can "provide training and credentialing for incumbent workers in healthcare and ... prepare new workers to succeed and meet the workforce demands for this sector – expanding individual opportunity and economic vitality."

Educating nurses is one of the most important contributions community colleges make to society. But programs that lead to an RN are expensive to run, and finding qualified instructors with a master's degree in nursing is challenging as these nurses can typically earn more money working in direct care. However, it is estimated that there will be 1.2 million job openings for RNs in the U.S. economy by 2020.

And there is already a pool of healthcare workers who have received certification to be LPNs, paramedics or medical assistants, and would benefit from a program dedicated to helping them to become RNs.

Community colleges can work with these individuals and collaborate with local hospitals to create or enhance career pathways for their employees. Partnerships with hospitals are key to training nurses, and offering clinical training at the workplace is vital to the success of these programs.

Community colleges often anticipate the need to provide training and contact healthcare providers to set up a program. That is the case with Portland Community College in Oregon, which created a certificate program for local assisted living centers, providing them with resident assistants responsible for helping residents undertake activities of daily living and maintain their emotional well-being, as well as avoiding falls, infections and skincare problems such as bedsores.

Other innovative programs created by community colleges for the healthcare industry include Renton Technical College in Seattle, training entry level workers at the Virginia Mason Medical Center to become medical assistants; Owensboro Community & Technical College helping individuals on the lower rungs of employment at the Owensboro Medical Health System - including nursing aides and pharmacy technicians - become RNs; and Bunker Hill Community College in Boston, creating a Community Health Worker Certificate that prepares low-income students to provide underserved neighborhoods with information about health issues and access to healthcare services.

At Ivy Tech in Indiana, we developed a Healthcare Specialist certification that leads to jobs in Dementia Care, Phlebotomy, Pharmacy Technician and Outpatient Insurance Coding. We work with local hospitals, pharmacies and clients to place our graduates in these positions as well as nurses, EMTs, physician's assistants among others.

What all these programs have in common is that community colleges worked with healthcare providers to train their employees offering them flexible hours, on the job training, mentors and accelerated degree programs. These innovative programs lead directly to pay raises and career advancement.

The healthcare sector offers well-paying jobs and opportunities for advancement. Jobs can't be shipped overseas and communities depend on quality health care. Community colleges are on the front lines in training America's healthcare professionals, and will continue to serve our growing healthcare needs.

Community colleges are proactively creating apprenticeship programs that lead to well-paying jobs in the factories of the future.

22 – APPRENTICESHIP PROGRAMS: AN AGE-OLD ANSWER FOR CONTEMPORARY NEEDS

January 3, 2016

Apprenticeships, where young people learned skills on the job from a master craftsman such as a stone cutter, have been around since the Middle Ages. An apprentice would earn while he learned and often lived with the journeyman providing the training.

In the early days of this country, apprentices were indentured servants. Ben Franklin was an indentured servant to his older brother, who taught him the printing trade The advent of the Industrial Revolution brought with it a greater demand for skilled craftsmen and most of these workers began their careers as apprentices.

Today, community colleges are proactively creating apprenticeship programs that lead to well-paying jobs in the factories of the future, where proficiency in computer science has replaced the repetition of the assembly line. They are looking for opportunities to implement curricula with local manufacturers to train their workforce, many of whom have decades on the job, in the skills that will see them through the rest of their careers.

In 2014, the U.S. Department of Labor announced $100 million in grant opportunities that would fund apprenticeship programs in high-growth industries such as health care, advanced manufacturing and information technology. Apprenticeship programs are one surefire way to revitalize the middle class, and with it, the American Dream.

Today's apprenticeship programs are based on a successful German model where high school students opt to work while they learn in return for a highly skilled factory job when they complete their apprenticeship. Replicating the German apprenticeship system in the United States requires a cultural shift. We view late adolescence as a time of exploration, and higher education to be broad and inclusive, when it's often more appropriate to be instilling skills that will launch a lucrative and satisfying career.

Apprenticeships are more narrowly defined than a liberal arts degree, but at a time when student debt exceeds $1.2 trillion, we need to explore other avenues and focus more on employment opportunities, which apprenticeships provide, rather than clinging dogmatically to a belief that everyone should attend a four-year college. The Department of Labor estimates that 87 percent of apprentices are fully employed after they finish their programs, and the average starting salary is $50,000.

By contrast, the average starting salary for someone from the class of 2014 with a fresh liberal arts/general studies degree was $29,000 according to the Georgetown University Center on Education and the Workforce.

German companies such as Siemens with plants in the U.S. were among the first to institute the German apprenticeship system in communities where they have a presence. Siemens pays for its apprentices to attend Central Piedmont Community College while working at its Charlotte, N.C., plant.

Students split their time between the classroom and the Siemens factory that builds steam and natural gas-fired turbines for power plants around the world. The apprenticeships follow a rigorous curriculum that leads to an Associate degree in mechatronics, a hybrid discipline created by Japan and Germany that melds the basics of mechanical engineering, electronics and other relevant areas.

Students coming out of this program can program, operate and fix machines common in the factories run by Siemens and other top companies. These are jobs that cannot be shipped overseas. Siemens estimates that it costs around $160,000 for it to train an apprentice. This includes tuition, books and wages paid during the three-and-a-half year program.

Other German companies have instituted apprenticeship programs at their U.S. plants. The Volkswagen Academy at Chattanooga State Community College in Tennessee is a three-year program that combines five semesters of academic and practical training with four semesters of paid, on-the-job training. Students are taught at the state-of-the-art Academy adjacent to the VW's plant in South Carolina. BMW and Bosch also have plants in Tennessee and run similar apprenticeship programs.

But it is not just German companies that are instituting apprenticeship offerings in conjunction with community colleges. American manufacturers are also creating these programs.

Kellogg Community College in Battle Creek, Michigan, has apprenticeship programs that are sponsored by local companies, at which prospective students apply for an apprenticeship position. The programs are generally four years long and consist of 8,000 hours of paid on-the-job training and a minimum of 576 hours of related classroom instruction. There are programs in machine technology, industrial technology, electricity and electronics, among others.

Tidewater Community College in Norfolk, Va., has a unique apprentice program with the Norfolk Naval Shipyard. Apprentices are employed with a salary range of $13.84 to $15.26 per hour and receive promotions upon successful completion of program requirements. Students participate in a rigorous training schedule that combines academic classes at the college along with trade theory training and on-the-job experience. Honolulu Community College has a similar program with Pearl Harbor Shipyard.

In Indiana, Ivy Tech has apprenticeship programs with the Indiana Union Construction Industry, where students receive approximately 2,000 hours of on-the-job training and a minimum of 216 hours of classroom instruction every year. First-year union apprentices earn about the same amount that most college students pay for a year's tuition. Graduates can earn up to $60,000 annually. There are programs for boilermakers, bricklayers, carpenters and electricians. In addition, Ivy Tech works with local manufacturers such as Chrysler, ALCOA, Rolls Royce, and Cummins, among others, to educate these companies' future workforce.

Most apprenticeship programs require students to take rigorous national certification exams so they can work at any manufacturing facility in the country with their degree or certification.

If people knew the facts, we could change the mindset in this country that everyone should receive a four-year degree. Many parents, particularly those who didn't attend college, want more for their children than a job in a factory. But perhaps that is exactly what it best for a particular young person. And as a country, having enough people trained in the skills that apprenticeships provide could keep many jobs from going overseas. We should commit ourselves to apprenticeship programs. As one student said to me: "Apprenticeship was my golden ticket to the middle class."

A FOUNDATION FOR HIGHER EDUCATION

Today there are many paths to a solid
education, and increasingly community
college is taking precedence. Almost half of
those who graduate from a four-year college
have a two-year college on their transcripts as
well, according to a 2015 report from the
National Student Clearinghouse Research
Center. Community colleges also specialize
in supporting those who need remedial
courses or other readiness preparation to
handle college-level work.

Graduation rates for students transferring after receiving an Associate degree are higher than for those who went directly to four-year institutions.

23 – COMMUNITY COLLEGES AND COLLEGE ATTAINMENT

October 14, 2013

President Obama has set a new goal for the country: that by 2020, America would once again have the highest proportion of college graduates in the world.

We have a lot of work to do in order to achieve this. For the past 20 years, the United States has been stuck at a 38 percent college attainment level. Compare this number to Korea, where 60 percent of the population holds a higher education degree or certificate.

Community colleges have made college attainment a priority. At Ivy Tech in Indiana, the nation's largest singly-accredited community college system, we have launched the "Complete College Indiana," which focuses on the role we will play in increasing the state's current college attainment rate of 33 percent. Ivy Tech serves 47 percent of public higher education enrollment in the state.

We are focusing on a number of key areas, among them enrolling high school students in dual-credit programs with Ivy Tech and helping adults with dead-end jobs or manufacturing skills that are now obsolete re-engineer themselves by going back to school.

To do this, we promote the fact that we have both day and evening courses six days a week, as well as online courses. We are also working closely with Indiana businesses to train their future workforce. While Indiana has lost manufacturing jobs, the manufacturing base is still strong, but requires a higher level skill set than the assembly lines of the past. Without skilled workers, these jobs will be outsourced overseas.

Other community colleges around the country have responded to the President's challenge with innovative programs. Northeast Alabama Community College has imitated the PASS program (Pathway for Achieving Student Success) designed to increase completion rates in their nursing program. Students enrolled in the two year nursing program take seminars on test-taking skills, study skills, time management and learning styles. Student progress is monitored throughout the nursing program. The faculty became involved in addressing the educational and psychosocial needs of the students. This very hands-on approach resulted in a retention rate that increased to 71 percent in 2011 from 28 percent in 2009.

Truckee Meadows Community College in Reno, Nevada, began its "Success First" program to help low-income, first-time, full-time, first-generation students. These students comprise 40 percent of the school's enrollment. Recognizing that these students may not be well-prepared for college level work, the college instituted a course that enabled them to adjust to a college environment with tips for reading, studying, note-taking, test-taking, and time management. Daily tutoring is available. Something as simple as providing lunch and textbooks allows students to focus on studying rather than worrying about how to pay for essentials. Students sign a contract at the beginning of the school year that indicates they understand what is required of them. One interesting outcome of "Success First" is that it creates a natural cohort of students who serve as a peer support group throughout their college career.

Community colleges need to be innovative because their students face many obstacles, among them the fact that many hold jobs or have family responsibilities. Virginia Community College System began the Shared Services Distance Learning to allow instructors to share their online courses with students from other partner colleges. More options mean that students experience less of a delay in getting the credits they need. Online education is not for everyone. However, it is an attractive option for community college students as it allows them the freedom of attending college without having to be on campus. The Virginia Community College System now offers 52 courses online.

Many high school students and adults need to stay in their community and don't have the option of packing up and moving to attend a four-year residential college. The majority are from low-income backgrounds and many are African American or Hispanic. Community colleges are in the vanguard of serving these students.

We are also sending more students on to four-year institutions. According to a 2012 report by the National Student Clearinghouse Research Center, graduation rates for students transferring after receiving an Associate degree are higher than for those who went directly to four-year institutions. Close to 71 percent of these students earned a bachelor's degree within four years and nearly 80 percent either graduated or persisted at a four-year institution.

Some may see the President's goal of America becoming the world leader in college education by 2020 as very ambitious. Community colleges know that the education they provide changes lives and will continue to develop programs that help students get a degree. We believe that the goal is attainable.

Research indicates that these jobs will be concentrated in healthcare, community services, STEM (Science, Technology, Engineering and Mathematics) and information technology – all areas where community colleges excel, offering either Associate degrees or certificate programs.

24 – RESEARCH SUPPORTS WORK OF COMMUNITY COLLEGES

July 29, 2013

When I was writing my book, *The Community College Career Track: How to Achieve the American Dream without a Mountain of Debt,* I came across the research of Dr. Anthony Carnevale, Director of the Georgetown University Center on Education and the Workforce. The Center's research focuses on the link between education, career qualifications, and workforce demands.

Dr. Carnevale's research confirms what community colleges have known for years. There are well-paying jobs available for applicants with an Associate degree or perhaps even completion of a certificate program. With student loan debt rising and unemployment high for recent graduates, students, parents, teachers, and guidance counselors should look to their local community college before enrolling in an expensive four-year school.

The Center's latest report, *http://cew.georgetown.edu/recovery2020/*, notes that the U.S. employment market will grow from 140 million to 165 million jobs by 2020. There will be 55 million job openings, of which 24 million will be newly-created positions and 31 million will be the result of the retirement of baby boomers.

The study also projects that 65 percent of job vacancies will require some post-secondary education and training. But not all of these positions will demand a bachelor's degree. Seven million jobs will only require an Associate degree and five million more will be filed by those with postsecondary certificate.

This is good news for community colleges. Many community colleges around the country are already working with local businesses to meet future workforce needs Dr. Carnevale's research indicates that these jobs will be concentrated in healthcare, community services, STEM (Science, Technology, Engineering and Mathematics) and information technology – all areas where community colleges excel offering either Associate degrees or certificate programs.

In a separate report, "Certificates: Gateway to Gainful Employment and College Degrees," Dr. Carnevale's team of economists pointed out the value of certificates, which have skyrocketed more than 800 percent over the past 30 years. Community colleges have always recognized the value of such programs, which can include certification in auto mechanics, drafting, electronics, police and protective services, healthcare, information services, transportation and agriculture.

The report also noted that high school graduates receive a 20-percent wage premium from a certificate. A median worker with a high school diploma earns slightly more than $29,000 while certificate holders earn slightly less than $35,000. This can mean the difference between living at the poverty level and a middle class life for a family. Over the past couple of years, certificate programs have become very popular with displaced workers. It enables them to be on the fast track in obtaining new skills and getting back into the workforce.

Perhaps the best thing about certificate programs is that a student can usually go through a community college program, spending less than $6,000 for coursework that is often covered by a Pell Grant.

Community college presidents around the country are following Dr. Carnevale's research closely in order to be better prepared to serve the future workforce. He estimates that the United States will fall short by 5 million workers with post-secondary education – at the current production rate – by 2020.

We need to recognize that not everyone should attend a four-year institution. There are good jobs available for those with a community college degree or graduates of a certificate program.

High school students should explore what certifications or degrees local businesses are looking for and begin tailoring their education to meet these criteria.

25 – HIGH SCHOOL STUDENTS SHOULD EARN CREDITS AT COMMUNITY COLLEGES

January 8, 2013

As higher education becomes more expensive, prospective students should take advantage of a great way to cut costs by taking college courses in high school.

An ideal way to accomplish this is to enroll in special programs set up by community colleges. By doing this, high school students can determine how ready they are to undertake a degree in higher education and, in some cases, save a considerable amount of money towards an associate or bachelor's degree.

According to the American Association of Community Colleges, the number of students, under the age of 18 enrolled in community-college courses, <u>rose</u> more than 50 percent in the past 10 years. For the 2011-12 academic year, there are now more than 800,000 high school students taking community college classes. Almost all of the more than 1,000 community colleges offer these dual enrollment programs.

Unlike Advanced Placement courses in high school, where a student often needs a pre-determined grade point average to enroll, courses at community colleges are open to everyone. Students, who may not excel in English, for example, could do well in an automotive technology course.

Around the country, manufacturers have job openings that demand very specific skill sets. Many community colleges are now partnered with these businesses to meet their workforce needs. High school students should explore what certifications or degrees local businesses are looking for and begin tailoring their education to meet these criteria. Taking courses leading to a degree in healthcare is also a good way to getting an education that leads directly to a well-paying job.

At Ivy Tech in Indiana, where I have served as president since 2007, students can take courses at their high school for college credit once they have provided scores from PSAT, SAT or Accuplacer exams.

There is no charge for to enroll in an Ivy Tech course taught in a high school classroom by a qualified high school teacher. High school students also have the option of paying for a course taught at one of our many campuses throughout Indiana at night or on the weekend.

For high school students, who may be the first in their family to attend college, taking a course at a community college introduces them to the rigor of college coursework. Many community colleges offer these courses at a reduced rate. Taking these college courses enables high school students to accelerate their way through college and save money while doing so.

With student loan debt passing the $1 trillion mark, students need ways to earn a degree without incurring a mountain of debt. Starting college in high school is a good first step in that direction.

Free community college is a genuine opportunity to thwart the looming social and economic crisis that an uneducated America will otherwise face.

26 – FREE COMMUNITY COLLEGE IS A GAME CHANGER

January 9, 2015

President Obama's proposal to make community colleges free of charge is a bold initiative and a game changer for our country when it comes to educational attainment.

Just as FDR did in 1944 with the GI Bill and Lyndon Johnson's support of Pell Grants in 1965, a free community college system will offer access to higher education for millions and make possible getting a two-year degree that leads to a well-paying job or an affordable four-year option.

Naysayers will claim there is no money on the federal or state level to support the president's plan. But we must go beyond viewing free community college as a handout and rather see it as an investment in our country's future.

Community colleges train our police, firefighters, nurses, electricians, computer technicians, welders and chefs. Unlike graduates of four-year institutions, community college graduates usually have roots in local cities and towns and contribute to the local economy after they receive their degree.

We face a skills gap in this country and community colleges hold the solution. Hundreds of community colleges now partner with local businesses to train their workers for well-paying jobs that require advanced skills in new technologies. Some have embraced the apprenticeship system created in Germany where individuals learn both in the classroom and on the job.

In order to prevent manufacturing companies from moving their operations overseas it is imperative that we effectively train the American workforce. Many of these jobs require only a certificate that is nationally recognized and can be obtained in less than a year. We also need to retrain our displaced workers by giving them new skills that guarantee a living wage.

A free community college system also addresses the problem of student loan debt, which now totals $1.2 trillion. Taking core courses at a community college and then matriculating to a four-year institution would save students thousands of dollars. It is not just lower-income students that are shut out of higher education because of runaway costs at both our public and private institutions. The American middle class is also economically stymied when faced with the prospect of attending a four-year institution and amassing more than $80,000 in debt.

The president's plan is based on Tennessee's free community college program, which has been made available to students graduating high school this year. The Tennessee Promise program has received overwhelming support with more than 58,000 applicants representing 90 percent of the state's high school seniors. Our young people are desperate to receive a degree in higher education because they know it is a sure way to escape from poverty and a road map to achieving the American dream.

We need to move beyond bi-partisan politics and embrace the idea of a free community college system, an idea I believe will capture the imagination of the American people. It is a genuine opportunity to thwart the looming social and economic crisis that an uneducated America will otherwise face.

I strongly believe that guiding students through the transfer process is one of the core missions of the community college.

27 – COMMUNITY COLLEGES MISSION TO TRANSFER STUDENTS TO FOUR-YEAR INSTITUTIONS

January 20, 2016

It is vitally important for all community colleges to have a program in place that enables its students to transfer all of their credits to a four-year institution.

Community college students are often the first in their family to attend college. Navigating the maze of taking coursework that will readily transfer to a four-year public or private institution is the key to their success. But providing counselors and mentors is often too costly and many of these students fall through the cracks and never earn even an associate degree.

The result is often that a community college student will find himself taking 10 or 15 additional (and expensive) credit hours at a four-year school because that college or university will not accept classes taken at a two-year school. This could amount to as much as $10,000 in additional tuition costs.

Every community college needs to address this problem. Why should our students be penalized and made to pay thousands of dollars more in tuition and an investment of time they quite frankly don't have to get a four-year degree?

At Ivy Tech, the nation's largest singly-accredited community college system, we have divided the school into four divisions, and one of those is the university/transfer division. Students know from the moment they step onto our campus what coursework leads directly to a seamless transfer to one of Indiana's public universities.

We also have a successful program with Strayer University, an online school that is a realistic choice for our 75,000 nontraditional students who balance work and family obligations while they attend school. We have separate articulation agreements with a number of schools in Indiana to address the fact that they may not accept all the credits earned at Ivy Tech. Students should also be able to enroll at a four-year college before earning their associate degree and earn that degree through what is called a reverse transfer.

I strongly believe that guiding students through the transfer process is one of the core missions of the community college. Florida is a good example of how institutions of higher education operate as a single entity. If you have an associate of arts degree and an acceptable GPA level, you are guaranteed a spot in a four-year state institution and all of your credits are accepted.

Accrediting and government bodies need to look at Florida as a model for what other states should do for community college students. One way is for the government to step in and make transfer agreements a requirement for Pell grant money. As the majority of community college students have Pell Grants, no state wants to be in danger of losing this essential funding.

Ivy Tech has about 30,000 students each semester who are enrolled in transfer programs. Each year we're transferring literally half of them. But we need to do better along with other community colleges and four-year schools. We should instill in our students the importance of a two-year degree and how it serves as a stepping stone to a bachelor's degree. Their level of attainment will have an impact on their future earning potential. We should do everything possible to help them achieve.

High school students should enroll in dual-credit programs with their local community college so they become familiar with college-level courses and are able to bypass remedial courses.

28 – REMEDIAL EDUCATION AT COMMUNITY COLLEGES

December 21, 2015

According to the report, "Higher Education's Bridge to Nowhere," fifty-one percent of all applicants to community colleges are required to take remedial courses so they are prepared for college-level work.

Non-traditional students, who are older and may be out of school for more than 20 years, often find that they too must enroll in remedial courses after scoring in the lower percentile of the ACCUPLACER exam.

This is a problem faced by many community colleges. The nationwide cost of this remedial instruction is estimated at $4 billion a year.

Students must use the money they receive from Pell Grants or other sources of financial aid to pay for remedial courses. The courses don't count toward a degree. What almost inevitably happens is that these students become discouraged and drop out of school.

We need to solve this problem, and one way is to design courses that have a remedial component, but with credit hours. With these courses, students receive regular instruction three days a week and for the other two they receive embedded tutoring. Thus, there is no need for a student to languish in the limbo of remedial education.

Another program involves working with local high schools and having them administer the ACCUPLACER exam to juniors to address academic deficiencies before college. In addition, high schools should encourage all students to take four years of math, as pursuing a degree in STEM (Science Technology, Engineering and Math) is where the Labor Department projects there will be the best career opportunities. STEM jobs will all require a mastery of math.

Another issue facing high school students is to consider which math courses to take in preparation for college. Most are placed in high school algebra pathways when statistics or quantitative math would be more appropriate to prepare them for their chosen programs of study and careers.

Wherever possible, high school students should enroll in dual-credit programs with their local community college so they become familiar with college-level courses and are able to bypass remedial courses.

Non-traditional students, in particular, should be given an opportunity to study for the exam. There are free online resources like the Khan Academy, MyMathLab and MyMath Test that allow students to practice math problems in a variety of math subjects and areas.

All students should be encouraged to enter specific programs of study when they first enroll, rather than waiting to take courses for their majors. Research shows that students are twice as likely to graduate if they complete at least three courses in their chosen programs of study in their first year on campus. This keeps students from taking unnecessary coursework that lengthens the time it takes for them to graduate.

(It should be noted that 30 percent of students who complete their remedial courses don't even attempt their gateway courses within two years. They become discouraged with higher education.)

African American, Hispanic and a lower-income student should be particularly wary of being headed toward the remediation dead-end. The very students we want to help most can find themselves trapped in remedial courses.

I believe that mentoring programs are invaluable to helping prospective community college students navigate the admissions process so they have a clear idea of what they need to succeed. Many community college students are the first in their family to attend college. Signing up for classes can be daunting. Mentors can illuminate for them a clear path to success.

With many states looking at the possibility of free community college, the debate about who is prepared for college coursework will intensify. We need to start with local high schools to make sure that all students are on the college track, not just high achievers. High school students also need to know that they don't have to get an associate degree, but many times can earn a certificate that will lead to a well-paying job in careers such as court reporting or medical coding.

There should be no barriers to success in higher education, but sometimes the things we do to help people don't work out as planned. Mentoring and good high school guidance can help clear the way.

COMMUNITY COLLEGES AND THE ECONOMY

For every dollar a student spends on community college, he or she will earn an incremental $4.80 above expected earnings without that education, says a study by Economic Modeling Specialists International for the American Association of Community Colleges. U.S. society as a whole will see $1.1 trillion added to the economy as a result of the added productivity of those who have studied at a community college.

*Our faculty members come from the community
and are often small business owners themselves.
They know exactly what it takes to succeed.*

29 – COMMUNITY COLLEGES SUPPORT ENTREPRENEURS

April 9, 2014

S mall businesses account for 64 percent of the net new jobs created between 1993 and 2011 or 11.8 million of the 18.5 million net new jobs, according the Small Business Administration. Yet the SBA also points out that after five years many of these businesses fail. Entrepreneurs are vitally important to a regional economy and community colleges are in the vanguard of providing services to support them. These schools have a long history of contributing to workforce development. They have expanded this effort to include entrepreneurial development and have been extremely successful.

The National Association for Community College Entrepreneurship maintains that community colleges have three key competitive advantages when it comes to working with entrepreneurs.

One, community colleges are skilled at experiential learning, which is essential to encouraging an entrepreneurial mindset. Support staff and faculty understand that entrepreneurs learn from experience and tailor coursework to meet this need. Second, community colleges are co-immersed deeply in their entrepreneurial ecosystems. Their faculty members are often entrepreneurs. They are already working closely with local businesses and can draw on these alliances to help other entrepreneurs.

Finally, community colleges are flexible when it comes to creating coursework in direct response to the needs of the local business community. If there is a local company that makes wind turbines, there will be a course at the community college that addresses how to repair them.

The Gayle & Bill Cook Center for Entrepreneurship at Ivy Tech in Indiana offers four academic tracks: Certificate, Technical Certificate, Associates of Applied Science and Non-Credit, all designed to address the different needs of entrepreneurs. Foundation courses include managing personal finance, the fundamentals of public speaking, financial accounting and introduction to microcomputers through accounting systems applications. The two-year degree program includes a business development course for creating a business plan. Many students opt for the two semester Certificate in

Entrepreneurship that provides aspiring entrepreneurs with the fundamental skills they'll need to own and operate a business.

Other community colleges have established partnerships with local business such as Wake Tech in North Carolina which partnered with Wells Fargo in 2010 to create the Wake Tech-Wells Fargo Center for Entrepreneurship. The Center pays special attention to women, Hispanic and other minority business owners by offering scholarships to those who need help getting their business off the ground. Wells Fargo believes that if communities prosper, its banks will prosper as well.

Bunker Hill Community College in Boston runs the Community Center for Entrepreneurship as an outreach site of the Massachusetts Small Business Development Center. In addition to coursework, the college provides an entrepreneurship library, referral services for financial assistance and mini-grants, free seminars and a student Entrepreneurship Club.

Metropolitan Community College in Nebraska offers coursework that emphasizes the skills an entrepreneur needs to know and attracts those interested in starting a business as well as assistance to those looking for advice on how to grow their business. Although the program was started in 2006, it is now the state's largest educational provider of entrepreneurship studies.

I believe that helping entrepreneurs is one of the most important roles of a community college. We have the experience of working with small businesses to develop coursework to help train their employees. Our faculty members come from the community and are often small business owners themselves. They know exactly what it takes to succeed. We also have relationships with local banks and know what they are looking for in a business plan.

So whether it is launching a food truck, licensing a daycare center or guiding a tech start-up, community colleges know how to nurture a budding entrepreneur and give him or her the tools to succeed.

Community colleges are now America's best hope for both lower and middle-class Americans, looking for an affordable education that leads to a well-paying job.

30 – COMMUNITY COLLEGES AND THE SKILLS GAP

February 24, 2015

With a four year, residential college costing more than $80,000, parents and students are looking more closely at the return on investment. President Obama recently spoke at Ivy Tech in Indiana, the nation's largest singly-accredited community college system in the country, about his proposal to make a community college education free for most students.

The President also addressed the importance of colleges having an alliance with local businesses to train their workers, particularly through apprenticeship programs and career education in fields that pay well, such as construction and technology. People may disagree about politics, but there is little dispute that the U.S. needs a better-educated workforce in order to succeed.

The first thing we need to do is address the skills gap in this country. Baby boomers are retiring and businesses are looking for workers who are trained in emerging technologies. This is a national trend.

According to the Indiana Department of Workforce Development, employers will have to replace an estimated 667,000 workers by 2022, and an additional 336,600 new jobs are projected for the same time frame.

In August of 2013, the Boston Consulting Group (BCG) released a study, "The U.S. Skills Gap: Could it Threaten a Manufacturing Renaissance." The report estimated that the present high-skills gap in the U.S. is currently 100,000 workers nationwide. The solution has often been to ship these well-paying jobs overseas.

Community colleges are ideally positioned with solutions for the skills gap. These schools can move quickly to establish curricula that precisely address local workforce development needs. Adjunct faculty are often also employed by local businesses, so they know exactly what skills employees need to get a job and advance through the ranks. Increasingly, community colleges are looking to create apprenticeships with local businesses so students can earn while they learn.

For students, there is also the option of enrolling in a certificate program. The Georgetown University Center on Education and the Workforce pointed out in a 2012 study that certificates are the fastest growing form of post-secondary credentials in the U.S. largely because they are affordable, take less than a year to complete and often yield high returns.

As the former CEO of Delco Remy International, a manufacturing company, I am acutely aware of the problems manufacturers face in hiring highly skilled workers. Our factories are run by the new "blue tech" workers, individuals with good math skills who can work with automated systems. Manufacturers now run quiet, smaller factories – a marked difference from the noisy, dirty assembly lines of the past. An entry-level position in one of these factories can pay as much as $50,000 a year.

At Ivy Tech, we created the Corporate College to provide workforce training solutions for the needs of businesses, organizations and individuals. We developed a partnership with Aisin USA Manufacturing to address the shortage of automation and robotics technicians. We worked with Barry Plastics Corporation with an apprenticeship program that trains more than 100 employees. Displaced and underemployed workers are trained by Carter Express Incorporated and Ivy Tech, representing a $4 million positive economic impact on the local community.

President Obama's proposal for a free community college education would work wonders for many people. But it's important to remember that even today, community colleges are very affordable resource. A two-year degree costs around $6,300, about a third of what it would run at a state-run four-year institution. In fact, community college tuition right now can be free for lower income students who qualify for Pell grants. But these students often struggle to pay for books, childcare and even gas in order to get a degree.

The President pointed out in his Ivy Tech speech that young people today may have three or four careers in their lifetime, and employers want them ready to produce from the get go. We can no longer rely on the luxury of on-the-job training. Employers expect that those they hire are thoroughly prepared, whether they be RNs or a welders. Community colleges get those employees ready to do their jobs.

Community colleges are now America's best hope for both lower and middle-class Americans, looking for an affordable education that leads to a well-paying job. Whatever we can do to increase access for more people will pay off for all of us in the end.

Community college students need an education that will enable them to work on an international level.

31 – COMMUNITY COLLEGES AND CHINA

December 21, 2015

In order to succeed in a global economy, college students need to be exposed to way different cultures work and get things done. That's why Ivy Tech in Indiana, the nation's largest singly-accredited community college system, has established a sister college relationship with Huzhou Vocational & Technical College in Huzhou, China. The college in China is located in one of the country's most developed economic hubs.

This new alliance will provide academic and cultural exchange opportunities that will greatly enhance the educational capabilities of both institutions. We deeply value partnerships that can strengthen our culture of providing meaningful opportunities to our students and faculty.

The partnership came about after a group of government, economic development and education officials from Indiana visited China. For Ivy Tech, our goal was to ensure that business leaders in China, considering locating or expanding their U.S. operations in Indiana, were aware that we can train their local workforce. Ivy Tech already provides training for major manufacturers in the state, and together we have created apprenticeship programs that enable our students to get paid while learning on the job.

Both colleges will cooperate on student/faculty exchange programs; collaborate on creating curricula and setting up distance learning programs; and partner on scientific research and innovation. We are also exploring providing students at both institutions with the opportunity to do one or more years of their education in China or the United States.

Ivy Tech and Huzhou offer programs in advanced automation robotics, computer information technology and engineering technology. All of these fields provide excellent career paths with manufacturing companies.

We are already seeing that community college students need an education that will enable them to work on an international level. In today's global economy, partnering with a Chinese technical college will ensure that Ivy Tech students know what kind of training is necessary to work with Chinese companies, and have access to the curricula that will help their careers.

Community colleges have the ability to respond quickly to fulfill the workforce needs of local businesses. It is my hope that international corporations looking to open facilities in the United States will view community colleges as partners in workforce development.

China is just the beginning.

When opportunities come along for economic development, towns and small cities frequently turn to the local community college to help them plan, prepare the workers, and give them a competitive edge.

32 – THE CONTRIBUTIONS OF COMMUNITY COLLEGES TO CITIES AND TOWNS

September 18, 2015

In many small cities and towns, community colleges are more than educational institutions. They function as civic centers, host wedding receptions and offer free cultural events.

Local businesses rely heavily on community colleges for workforce development. Cape Cod Community College contacted a group of regional startup companies and created an associate degree in engineering. The school also predicted that energy efficiency and renewable energy would be key industries for the area. Three certificate programs were launched in photovoltaic, thermal and wind technology to train workers for the rapidly expanding renewable energy industry.

Wine is one of the fastest growing industries in Washington state. Yakima Valley Community College created associate degrees in viticulture and enology. The college also opened a teaching winery and two winery incubators – two startups that offer students on-the-job experience.

Rural communities depend upon their community colleges to train healthcare professionals. Lewis and Clark Community College in Godfrey, Illinois created the Nurse Managed Center providing valuable experience for students studying for an RN degree. The Center provides an important link between the academic program and clinical experience in a Center staffed by nurse practitioners. There is also a mobile health unit to bring services to remote corners of the state.

The city of Terre Haute, Indiana, reached out to Ivy Tech Community College as part of its effort to receive seed money for workforce development projects. A finalist in the America's Best Communities competition, Terre Haute received $50,000 to work with Ivy Tech and others to develop a comprehensive strategy to improve the city's economy and quality of life. The competition was created by Frontier Communications to help rural communities compete for more than $10 million in prize money. Terre Haute has a chance for one of the top prizes ($3 million, $2 million, and $1 million), which would put that strategy effectively to work.

Unlike students in other college towns, individuals, getting a degree or certification at a community college, usually stay there. They become the city's police officers, nurses, firefighters and chefs.

Many high school students enroll at a community college in their senior year to get academic credit at a reduced price. These courses can then be applied to their freshman year at a community college or a four-year institution.

Community colleges are integral and important partners with local municipalities. The positive town-gown relations are pivotal to these institutions.

So when opportunities come along for economic development, towns and small cities frequently turn to the local community college to help them plan, to prepare the workers, and to give them a competitive edge. I'm rooting for Terre Haute, and I'll bet there are 49 other community college leaders hoping that the winners of America's Best Communities will be some of their own.

The skills gap in this country can be addressed –
and free community college is one way – to train
the workers of the future.

33 – INVESTING IN THE AMERICAN WORKFORCE

September 29, 2015

A recent poll conducted by the Gallup-Lumina Foundation found that while Americans may be politically polarized, they all agree that the United States needs to invest in the talent of its workforce. Talent is defined as "the knowledge or skills people develop or obtain through education, work or other life experiences."

As an estimated 10,000 baby boomers reach retirement age every day, employers across sectors are competing for experienced candidates from a fast-shrinking talent pool. Those polled by Gallup agreed that, "the federal government should make it a high priority to increase the talent of our nation's workforce." And 89 percent agreed with the statement that cities must commit to increasing talent among their citizens in order to have "stronger economies, better quality of life and greater prosperity."

There is also widespread consensus among various demographic groups. When asked if the federal government should step in and make increasing the talent of the nation's workforce a priority, there was no difference in opinion among racial groups (87 percent of whites and 88 percent of nonwhites agree) and income groups (89 percent of households making less than $24,000 a year and 89 percent of households making more than $90,000 agree).

What is most significant is the role higher education plays in this discussion. There is strong support for "redesigning the nation's higher education system to better meet students' needs as a means to increase the country's talent pool. "

This poll confirms what community colleges have known for decades: Americans view higher education as essential to economic prosperity for their cities and towns. Many jobs now require some college education or a completion of a certificate program that enables students to practice a trade, become an EMT or work in the hospitality industry, among others.

We need continued partnerships with local businesses to train the workforce. Many community colleges meet regularly with the business community to create curriculum that accomplishes this. In some instances, the colleges hire employees from these businesses to work as adjunct professors.

These companies also provide apprenticeships so that students can earn while they learn. Ivy Tech in Indiana has done this for years with our manufacturing companies.

Community colleges should be part of a team of civic leaders, politicians, and business leaders that reaches out to manufacturing companies looking to re-locate or a build a new factory. This partnership will prevent companies from shipping their plants overseas.

High school guidance counselors should encourage motivated students to take courses at community colleges in their senior year. These courses are recognized by both the local community college as well as many four-year institutions. They also reduce student debt.

The skills gap in this country can be addressed – and free community college is one way – to train the workers of the future.

The Gallup-Lumina Foundation poll found that both Democrats (90 percent) and Republicans (89 percent) agree that cities committed to increasing talent among their citizens are more likely to have a stronger economy.

We need to put our political differences aside and work together as a country to strengthen our economy by investing in education. America once beat the world in innovation, creating entrepreneurs and economic growth. By getting down to business and developing our workforce, we can do so once again.

AFTERWORD

I didn't set out to become an educator, much less president of Indiana's Ivy Tech, the largest singly-accredited community college system in the country. In my previous life, I was CEO of Delco Remy, an $8 billion manufacturer of auto parts and once a division of General Motors.

But from those many years in industry, I learned just how important the proper education and training were to America and its manufacturing base, especially as technology became increasingly essential on the factory floor. It was no longer enough for an employee to just have the basics; setting up and operating machines now require advanced language and mathematics skills.

Excellent communications were needed for advanced manufacturing processes such as just-in-time scheduling and kaizen, the cooperative inclusion of everyone in the organization to work together with utmost efficiency, and solve problems themselves and with their peers. Continuous improvement and six-sigma quality programs required the ability to understand and work with algebra and statistics.

The place where such skills could be taught best was often right down the road, at the local community college, which was nimble enough to customize programs for employers, quick to the market with new curricula and could offer courses at times and in places that other educational institutions would find impossible.

And community colleges could do it at a very low cost, compared to most other schools.

Through my years at Ivy Tech, I sought to hone this model, make it work for an increasing number of students (and employers), and to educate and change minds about what community colleges could do for Americans and the American economy. I thought much about what Ivy Tech and I were doing, and sought to share my ideas and practices with other, both in and outside of the education sector.

The essays on the preceding pages collect much of my thinking, and I hope some genuine insights, about how to align community colleges and our economy even more closely. I believe that community colleges are the answer to many of our problems in growing and keeping jobs, preserving the middle class, and giving Americans a secure and rewarding future.

I am proud of the many thousands of students who studied at Ivy Tech during my tenure, whether it was to achieve an Associate degree, prepare for a four-year college, earn a technical or professional certificate, or take a course or two to improve themselves personally or in their careers. Community college is a different animal than our traditional system, and its successful products, our students, are contributing greatly to our society and our economy.

As I close this book, the prospect of making community college free of cost for the great majority of students nationwide is a very real possibility. Though I will soon retire from Ivy Tech, I will continue my work to help make it so. I have seen the future in my community college work, and I know that if we treasure and utilize this magnificent, evolving resource, it will be very bright indeed.

Tom Snyder

FREQUENTLY ASKED QUESTIONS

Why do community colleges offer the best ROI in higher education? See Chapter 2: Questions for Your College of Choice

If I go to a community college, what kind of job can I get? See Chapter 1: Community college Success Stories

Why is an associate degree as important as a four year degree? See Chapter 3: Employers Should Value the Two Year Degree

What needs to be done to insure that community college students succeed? See Chapter 4: Supporting Community College Students

Should the United States make a significant investment in career and technical education? See Chapter 5: The Case for Career and Technical Education

Why is online education important to a community college student? See Chapter 6: The Benefits of Online Learning.

What types of programs do community colleges have to help low-income or first time students? See Chapter 7: A Better Way to Help Low-Income Students

How do community colleges work with veterans? See Chapter 8: Community Colleges and Returning Vet

Does it make sense to go back to school if you are 50 plus? See Chapter 9: Back to College at 50

What resources do community colleges offer the displaced worker? See Chapter 10: Community Colleges Welcome Career Changers

When does it make sense to enroll in a certificate program? See Chapter 11: Professional Certificates from a Community College – A Solution for the Unemployed.

Why are mentoring programs so important at community colleges? See Chapter 12: Mentoring Cultivates College Success

Why are community colleges a great resource for retired people? See Chapter 14: Retirees Return to Community College

How does one get in on the ground floor of aviation technology? See Chapter 15: The Booming Field of Aviation Technology.

Why is criminal justice a great field of study? See Chapter 16: Criminal Justice and Community College

What do you need to get a good job in the hospitality industry? See Chapter 17: The Hospitality Industry and Community College

Can community colleges contribute to a re-birth of American manufacturing? See Chapter 18: Community Colleges and the Manufacturing Sector

Why is the RN degree from a community college still important? See Chapter 19: A Threat to the Backbone of Our Healthcare System – Restricting Access to Nursing

How are community colleges capitalizing on the increase demand for tech support? See Chapter 20:

Community Colleges and Tech Support

How do community colleges prepare one for a degree in the burgeoning healthcare industry? See Chapter 21: Community College and Healthcare

What is an apprenticeship program? See Chapter 22: Apprenticeship Programs: An Age-Old Solution to a Contemporary Problem

What are community colleges doing to address college attainment in the United States? See Chapter 23: Community Colleges and College Attainment

What are some of the innovative programs at community colleges that are helping students get a degree? See Chapter 12: Mentoring Cultivates College Success; and Chapter 23: Community College and College Attainment

What do prominent researchers say about a community college education? See Chapter 24: Research Supports the Work of Community Colleges

What are dual enrollment programs? See Chapter 25: High School Students Should Earn Credits at Community Colleges

Why should states support free community college? See Chapter 26: Free Community College is a Game Changer

What are the pros and cons of remedial education? See Chapter 28: Remedial Education at Community College

What services do community colleges offer entrepreneurs? See Chapter 29: Community Colleges

Support Entrepreneurs

Why is the skills gap a national concern? See Chapter 30: Community Colleges and the Skills Gap

Should community colleges look for overseas partnerships? See Chapter 31: Community Colleges and China

How do community colleges help their cities and towns? See Chapter 32: The Contributions of Community Colleges to Cities and Towns

Why are community colleges so important to the United States economy? See Chapter 33: Investing in the American Workforce

How easy is it to transfer from a community college to a four year institution? See Chapter 27: Community Colleges' Mission to Transfer Students to Four-Year Institutions

Who goes to a community college? See Chapter 1: Community College Success Stories; Chapter 8: Colleges and Returning Vets; Chapter 9: Back to College at 50; and Chapter 14: Retirees Return to Community College

I wasn't a good student in high school. Can I succeed at community college? See Chapter 4: Supporting Community College Students; Chapter 28: Remedial Education at Community Colleges; and Chapter 12: Mentoring Cultivates College Success

Will a community college prepare me for a four-year degree? See Chapter 23: Community Colleges and College Attainment

How can my business work with the local

community college? See Chapter 29: Community Colleges Support Entrepreneurs; and Chapter 30: Community Colleges and the Skills Gap

My work schedule changes all the time. How can I fit in courses at a community college? See Chapter 6: The Benefits of Online Learning

I can't get a promotion at work unless I acquire new skills. How can a community college help me? See Chapter 11: Professional Certification from a Community College: A Solution for the Unemployed

I'm in a dead-end job. What should I do? See Chapter 10: Community Colleges Welcome Career Changers

My child is smarter than the courses she takes in high school, how can I help her meet her potential? See Chapter 25: High School Students Should Earn Credits at Community Colleges

Do I need a four-year college degree? See Chapter 5: The Case for Career and Technical Education

My son unfortunately doesn't want to go to college, how can I help guide him? See Chapter 22: Apprenticeship Programs: An Age-Old Solution to a Contemporary Problem

I want to hire the best people with the best preparation, but I'm skeptical of those who've gone to community college. What should I know? See Chapter 3: Employers Should Value the Two-Year Degree

My son is a tech geek. What would a community college have to offer him? See Chapter 20: Community

Colleges and Tech Support

Do community colleges offer opportunities to explore different fields? See Chapter 25: High School Students Should Earn Credits at Community Colleges

My company doesn't have much money to train workers. Can a community college help? See Chapter 30: Community Colleges and the Skills Gap; and Chapter 22: Apprenticeship Programs: An Age-Old Solution to a Contemporary Problem.

Do community college faculty members know their stuff? See Chapter 4: Supporting Community College Students; Chapter 2: Questions for Your College of Choice; Chapter 30: Community Colleges and the Skills Gap; and Chapter 24: Research Supports Community Colleges

I want my daughter to have opportunities I did not. Will community college help her? See Chapter 1: Community College Success Stories; and Chapter 24: Research Supports Work of Community Colleges

We don't have money to send our child to college. What can we do? See Chapter 2: Questions for the College of Your Choice; and Chapter 4: Supporting Community College Students.

ABOUT THE AUTHOR

Thomas J Snyder serves as president of Ivy Tech Community College, the largest institution of higher education in Indiana and the nation's largest singly-accredited statewide community college system

He is that rare breed among community college presidents in that he is not an academic. Snyder joined Ivy Tech in 2007, after a successful career as Chairman CEO/President of two manufacturing companies: Flagship Energy Systems Center and Delco Remy International, Inc. During his 11 years at the helm of Delco Remy, he established a new business model and diversified the former General Motors division from a $500 million automotive parts supplier to $1.3 billion in sales as a global leader in truck, off-road and aftermarket products with more than 6,000 employees worldwide.

Under Snyder's leadership, Ivy Tech has raised more than $170 million, including a $2.5 million Trade Adjustment Assistance Community College and Career Training grant for information technology and cyber security education. Other significant funding includes a $22.9 million Lilly Endowment Grant, the largest grant in the history of Ivy Tech. The grant was used to create a world class training center.

Along with significantly growing Ivy Tech's enrollment numbers, Snyder has launched student success pathways, added major new facilities and improved operational efficiencies. These initiatives have shown positive results, ranging from improved graduation rates to upgraded bond ratings from both Standard and Poor's and Fitch.

Ivy Tech is first in the nation among two-year colleges for the number of associate degrees granted in the 2013-14 school year. President Barack Obama cited Ivy Tech in 2015 as "one of the best in the country" during an official campus visit to outline his proposal for two years of free community college for all Americans.

Snyder was selected in September, 2015, by President Obama to serve on the College Promise Advisory Board, which brings together luminaries and leaders to share best practices and ideas for models to make community college free for all students and to serve as a way for those leaders to recruit more of their peers to join the cause.

He was also chosen by President Obama to serve on a Roundtable on Affordability and Productivity in Higher Education at the White House in December 2011. The roundtable included Secretary of Education Arne Duncan as well as senior White House advisors in discussions to explore effective practices that promote affordability and productivity in higher education.

In October, 2010, Snyder and Ivy Tech student Michael Rice were invited by Dr. Jill Biden to participate in the first-ever White House Summit on Community

Colleges. President Obama asked Dr. Biden to convene the event to highlight the critical role community colleges play in developing America's workforce. Ivy Tech subsequently hosted the largest regional U.S. Department of Education summit on community colleges in March 2011 as a follow up to the White House Summit on Community Colleges.

One of four college presidents invited to testify at a hearing on college affordability before the U.S. Health, Education, Labor and Pensions Committee, Snyder noted that Ivy Tech costs less, adjusted for inflation, than it did four years ago. By capping the number of required textbooks, providing more online courses and reducing overhead costs, Ivy Tech is one of the most economical options available in higher education.

Snyder graduated from Kettering University, formerly General Motors Institute, with a degree in mechanical engineering. He also holds a master's degree in business administration from Indiana University.

He currently serves on the boards of Conexus, Energy Systems Network, Lightweight Innovations for Tomorrow, Community College Advisory Panel , Auto Community Network, The Manufacturing Institute, Midwestern Higher Education Compact, Rebuilding America's Middle Class, Central Indiana Corporate Partnership, Indiana Career Council, Tocqueville Society of United Way, Academic Advisory Council, National Workforce Solutions Advisory Board, and the Paramount Theater.

10/20

33961037R00086

Made in the USA
San Bernardino, CA
15 May 2016